SWILL 2012

Neil Williams

Vile Fen Press

a division of Klatha Entertainment an Uldune Media company

SWILL 2012
Copyright © 2024 Neil Williams

Library and Archives Canada Cataloguing in Publication

Williams, Neil, 1958-
(Jamieson-Williams, Neil, 1958-)

   SWILL 2012 / Neil Williams.

ISBN 978-1-894602-31-0
   1. Science fiction--History and criticism.

2. Science fiction fans. I. Title.

PN3433.5.J36 2012   809.3'8762   C2012-901693-4

Previously published as SWILL @ 30: 2012
Copyright © 2024 Neil Williams
Neil Jamieson-Williams
ISBN 978-1-894602-25-9
PN3433.5.J36 2012   809.3'8762   C2012-901693-4

Published by Vile Fen Press
an imprint of Uldune Media
504 – 635 Canterbury Street,
Woodstock, ON, Canada, L4S 8X9.
www.uldunemedia.ca

Table of Contents

Introducing SWILL 2012

Not much change from SWILL 2011, really.

The cover is inspired by the Australian fictional character of Anti-Fan. Sort of a Guy Fawkes-esque figure, an evil plotter who is against all that is decent and good and wholesome in Australian fandom. Okay, in reality, he is just against any Australian bids to host Worldcon. Anti-Fan attempts to thwart and/or assassinate the Aussie Worldcon Bid Committee, and is foiled in his attempts.

Initially, I had zero knowledge that this cartoon figure was associated with the Aussiecon 1 bid back in the 1970s. I was aware of Anti-Fan's return with the 1983 bid (which Anti-Fan was successful in halting) as I was hanging out with some Aussies in Toronto and later in Vancouver. As the perpetrator of SWILL, some of the Aussies thought that I was a Canadian agent of Anti-Fan; except that I strongly supported their 1983 bid. The years went by and my memory of Anti-Fan faded into the deep storage of my mind. Until SWILL 2012.

I was trying to come up with an idea for the cover art and vaguely remembered Anti-Fan. I found to usable artwork to play with and thus, cast myself into the image of Anti-Fan, complete with a lit bomb.

SWILL 2012 also begins the series Taboos of Science Fiction.

Neil Williams
August 2024

TRIGGER WARNING

SWILL is written to BE OFFENSIVE. Really, this is one of the premeditated intents of SWILL. It was written to offend back forty years ago and also just twelve years back in time.

It was not written for the sensibilities of those people under 30 years of age in the mid 2020s.

If you are the type of person who becomes so very much traumatised, that you have to curl up into a ball in bed for a week, after watching an episode of Friends where Chandler Bing talks about his father. If you thus find the 1990s sitcom Friends too racist, sexist, homophobic, and transphobic to watch, and you believe in the core of your heart, that this television series should never, ever, be permitted to air again and that all of the recordings and mastertapes of the series MUST be destroyed so there is now no danger that you will ever encounter this television show ever in the future; then SWILL is definitely not for you.

SWILL is offensive to many. That is one of the main purposes of SWILL. Read at your own risk.

You have been warned.

#13   Spring 2012

Table of Contents

SWILL is published quarterly (Spring, Summer, Autumn, and Winter)
along with an annual every February - in other words, five times
per year.

SWILL

Issue #13 Spring 2012

Copyright © 1981 - 2012 VileFen Press

a division of Klatha Entertainment an Uldune Media company

swill.uldunemedia.ca

Editorial: Well, Some of it was True...

Neil Jamieson-Williams

Sci-Fi calling
And I was there too;
You know what they say,
Well some of it was true.[1]

I am now on the borderlands of "old fart" status; subjectively defined and usually requiring the holder of the status to have at least a chronological age of 60 or more, though for those who constantly harp about "the good old days" this status can be achieved in their forties. Which means, although I am not quite yet and "old fart"; I can certainly pass for one. It also means that I have "been around..."

As I briefly mentioned in a previous issue (#9 Editorial for the fannishly pedantic) I did not start reading science fiction with the juveniles; I began with adult science fiction in the form of Arthur C. Clarke, I then tried a little Asimov (which I didn't care too much for, e.g. the Foundation trilogy and I am one of those few heretics that consider The Gods Themselves to be his best novel), discovered Niven, had a brief taste of LeGuin (didn't like Rocannon's World - it was more like a fantasy than science fiction) but I wouldn't pursue her works further until about 1980 when I read The Dispossessed, then Ellison (which led me to Spinrad and Silverberg), and Malzberg (which lead me to Moorcock and the New Worlds writers), and so on. Along the way, I would be introduced to other authors by friends and fellow genre consumers/fans. Certain authors also wrote non-fiction, in particular from the list above, Ellison and LeGuin (and later, Malzberg) which would have a major influence on the development of the SWILL attitude.

True, Swill was begat as middle finger salute in response to the BNF reaction to the surreal prank of the Maplecon Slandersheet.

---

[1] Apologies to Joe Strummer...

Nevertheless, once Swill was initiated, my take[2] on the issues of science fiction and SF fandom was strongly influenced by the non-fiction writings of those three authors.

LeGuin and Ellison were my primary influences and it is from these authors that I received the notion that science fiction could be a powerful literary form, a form that could move beyond genre fiction. That the walls should come down between the genre ghettos and the literary mainstream, that science fiction should step beyond the ghetto walls and enter the community of literature. LeGuin would evoke this call in a mix of quiet academic tones and firm calls to the barricades; reason and emotion intermingled with action. Ellison was more like some doom-and-gloom homeless street preacher who's just had his megaphone all charged up again. Here we have similar ideas stated/screamed with anger and calls for retribution and declarations that the day of judgement is near and/or human extinction is imminent.

From both Ellison and Malzberg (with an occasional quip from LeGuin) I received the view that it was hopeless to expect that science fiction would ever live up to its full potential, to be the literature that it can be. The editors, the publishers, the development drones, the producers, the literary critics will never allow this come to pass. Nor will the fans. And as for the writers, they are as much to blame; due to self-censorship to the market, knee-jerk acceptance of the dominant viewpoint of the fans and the gatekeepers, and just simple fear. Science fiction already deals with the unknown, but it is far less reassuring to abandon all safety lines of genre convention and leap into the dark; it is even more fearful when one has no guarantee of receiving any acknowledgement for at least making the attempt and that there is a very strong probability that this fearless act will result in one being vilified, drawn and quartered, and labelled as publishable by both science fiction fandom and the gatekeepers of the genre. The very action of attempting to write science fiction as literature can be an act that is career destroying.

And so it goes… Ellison, LeGuin, and Malzberg have all written essays on the subject since the early 1980's, but the only insights are discussions on the growth of media SF. Their general collective opinion about media SF is very similar to that

---

[2] Which doesn't necessarily speak for Swill columnists such as Rainsford and Hoyt.

of many literary fans; if the misuse of science fiction's potential was the normative behaviour in the print medium, it is the second[3] most paramount goal in the electronic mediums. No hope, no enlightenment can be expected from these mediums; only possibly, but improbably, can the print medium offer a way through to the transition from commercial art to art.

Maybe, and maybe not. Point of context, all three of these writers are at least 20 years my senior - they come from the time period when the magazine was king, before the great collapse of the magazines in the late 1950's. They have strong memories of the genre as it was and as it developed in the late 1940's, through the 1950's, and into the 1960's. Not I, I was not there, yet. I cannot speak to this time period, the Golden Age and the emergence of New Wave. It would not be until 1969 when I entered the scene as a genre consumer. Thus, I became a genre consumer within the context that books not the magazines dominated print medium science fiction, the electronic mediums still did very little science fiction and most of it was of very poor quality, and the Golden Age was long gone and New Wave had already established itself. Thus, print was the major medium and the reader had an eclectic buffet to choose from. And choose I did, reading works well before I should have, e.g. *Beyond Apollo* and often not fully understanding the work. As I came of age, the New Wave was fading -- beaten back by a reactionary counter-Wave attempting to restore the Golden Age one more. While the New Wave was pushed to the margins, the goal of returning to the Golden Age failed.

Here we begin to see the emergence in science fiction that which has appeared within other art forms and throughout culture itself over the past thirty five years. The "fragmentation" bemoaned by fandom begins in the late 1970's - and not because of the rise of electronic media SF as is usually claimed. Electronic medium SF was still relatively sparse at that time, and most of it was banal; too banal to usurp print medium science fiction. No, the change began within the beloved print medium as the mass imploded under the counter-Wave reaction - never to re-appear. In the aftermath the sub-genres (always present in the past, but with less substantial form) manifested themselves as distinct and coherent entities; hard-science, soft-science, science fantasy, new space opera, military, alternate history, literary, etc. These distinct sub-genre entities grew slowly at first, then accelerating during the 1980's (assisted by the appearance of

---

[3] The primary goal being to make money at all costs.

cyberpunk[4]) and the true rise of electronic media SF), until by the late 1990's the stage has been set for the new millennium and the present. A present in which there is a fragmented genre of niche sub-genres and multiple mediums that are in themselves akin to sub-genres; a state that is not unique to science fiction itself but is dominant within the culture itself.

Can science fiction be a literature within this environment? Can there be literature at all? I believe that it can be, though the terms literature, literary, and genre may require some re-evaluation; fortunately, this has already been done. Outside of the ranks of the literati (the current critics of literature who write/present for the major media outlets) and academics of the discipline of English literature; the definition of these terms tend to be thus:

Literature is the art of the written word and can be categorised as poetry, fiction, and non-fiction. Our focus here shall be on fiction, which includes realistic fiction, non-realistic fiction, and faction (those works inspired by or based upon a true story). Depending upon who is creating up the categories, there are about 20 to 30 genres of fiction - many including sub-genres. The most pitiful hackwork and the works of whomever you view as being paramount in the cannon of English literature are all literature, period.

Genre is any category of fiction that tends to use a particular set of literary devices, tone, and content that identifies it as a unique and/or separate body of work within literature. Thus, the definition does not create a binary opposition of X is literature and Y is genre (therefore the work of troglodyte hacks); all fiction is written within a genre (and there about 10 genres within non-fiction).

Literary is the term used by - usually the literati - that defines what has been determined to be important and valid forms of literature. It is an elite definition that is intentionally exclusionary and marks a preference for realistic fiction within the genres of philosophical fiction, experimental fiction, satire, and the nonfiction novel - though it can and does include non-realistic fiction provided that it falls within one of these

---

[4] Which was not to everybody's liking. Cyberpunk was despised both by those longing for a return to the Golden Age and by those who were prominent within the New Wave movement itself, e.g. Ellison and Malzberg. In my opinion the cyberpunk movement was a kind of fusion between elements of the Golden Age and the New Wave. Regardless, cyberpunk is now dated and passé.

preferred genres. And it is a term that is used to exclude most of the genres within speculative fiction, as well as the majority of the other fiction genres within literature.

Is science fiction literary fiction? Sometimes, sometimes it is. Most of the time it isn't and most of the time neither are the majority of works written within the other genres of fiction. That is just the way things are. Does that mean that science fiction is sub-standard? The literati would quickly voice the affirmative and I would caution pause and reflection and context. When a took a few, very few, courses in English literature during my undergraduate degree, I was exposed to what was deemed the current exemplars of literary fiction - few of these works have entered into the cannon of "classics" of late 20th century literature; in fact, the majority are out of print and forgotten. What makes a work a literary classic, I think, is the skill of craft, combined with a mixture of unique/brilliant use of tone, voice, and literary device, that speaks - in some manner - to the human condition, and can continue to do so decades and/or centuries after it was written.

The definition of literary fiction is subjective and the majority of the present works that have been accorded this status will lose that status in the brief passage of a decade. They possess that status in the now only. Is most of literature, literary? No, it is not. As per Sturgeon's Revelation/Law, "That's because 90% of everything is crud." The quest for art is not safe, it is not secure, and it may not find a large audience. In the present world, the world of the multimedia conglomerates, art is potentially unprofitable and viewed as a barely respectable add-on. They want the sure thing, the guaranteed money-maker (and this is true whether or not you're talking about print or any other medium); if your work can satisfy that criteria and also be art, great. If it cannot, forget it. To paraphrase LeGuin, the quest for garbage never fails, but the quest for art will fail 90% of the time.

I have written hours of radio drama that I fully and honestly admit is crap[5] and I am proud of that work[6], nevertheless. Occasionally an episode or a week's run of episodes may possess

---

[5] On the Rocks Series 1 (5 minutes/250 episodes) and Series 2 (5 minutes/150 episodes) - a five day per week serial space opera set within the main asteroid belt.
[6] No so much for the quality, but for the sheer persistence of being able to write and produce these two series under tight time constraints and a very limited budget.

the odd glimmer of brilliance - but most of the time it was
rubbish. I have also written a few radio dramas that I am very
proud of that did not appeal to the audience here in Canada but
found an audience in Europe; dramas[7] that I still think to this
day are my best work in fiction. And I have written many others
that are mediocre to good, and that is that.

Science fiction can at times be literary and a lot of the time it
can be absolute shit or again to paraphrase LeGuin, just noise.
The same can be said for any other genre of literature, including
that most pretentious of genres, literary fiction. Is science
fiction a failed genre? Absolutely not. Does it live up to its
full potential; not often. Sometimes this does bother me, but it
does not bother me enough to scream obscenities from the street
corner or wallow in self-loathing. If nobody at all was
attempting work approaching art, I would actually care. But
there are enough writers who do make the attempt (and very often
they fail to pull it off; and some of them actually do accomplish
art). Yes, there are many writers who just grind out shit for
money (and some of that is at least mediocre); but, at the end of
the day, is this really such an awful thing? They know it is
hack work and we know it too - as consenting adults, perhaps
there is nothing wrong with that. Everybody needs some mindless
fluff now and again.

Because, what science fiction does best and when it is, I think,
the most artistic is not when it is invoking a sense of wonder,
but when it is summoning up the dread engines of the night. I
personally don't think that a steady diet of that material is
healthy for the soul - some occasional junk food is highly
recommended and fortunately, that is not in short supply.

---

[7] By the Shores of the Tranquil Sea (55 minutes/1 episode) and The Time Tracks
Set (45 minutes/6 episodes).

Thrashing Trufen: A Thorough Tolchocking

Neil Jamieson-Williams

1.   **tolchock**
n. Nadsat slang meaning: a swing or blow

   A. Quit throwing tolchocks at me fanzine!
   B. A tolchock to the yarbles hurt him badly.

2.   **tolchock**
v. Nadsat slang meaning: to beat or strike another person
   A. We were about to tolchock the starry Trekkie when the millicents arrived.
   B. He tolchocked the article and razrezzed the rest of the fanzine into malenky bits.

There will be no waffling, no attempt to give any benefit of any doubt, no boilerplate that this refers to some-but-not-all -- science fiction fans can be self-inflated, troglodytic, provincial, back-biting, cowardly assholes. For some fans, this is simply their factory default setting. For the majority of fans, they are assholes some of the time. Is this some great and wonderful insight on my part; of course not. It is a simple deduction based on the following sources; what SF writers have said about their audience (fans), what fans have written about themselves (fan histories, fanzines, blogs), and personal experience (for the most part recollections).

Let's begin with the writers, shall we. I will limit the field to those whose essays on science fiction, which often sidebar into science fiction fandom, I know well: Harlan Ellison, Ursula K. LeGuin, and Barry N. Malzberg.

Ellison pulls no punches; he has open contempt for most SF fans and for good reasons too. Fans don't know boundaries; fans don't believe that writers should receive a liveable level of compensation for their work, fans think that they know more about a writer's stories than the writer does, that fans lack sophistication, fans are middle-class (with a tendency toward lower middle-class) bozos, fans insist upon placing authors on a pedestal only so that they can knock them down, fans read any perceived or real negative traits in an author's fictional characters as evidence of the writer's own personality flaws, and so on. He has also said many other negative things about science fiction fans over the years and most of it justifiable. And then there is the elevator story -- this undying tale is the SF fan urban myth that the evil Ellison threw an annoying fan down the elevator shaft at (I think, the 1974) Worldcon in Washington, D.C. It never happened. Then again, we are talking about Harlan Ellison -- the self-appointed gadfly of speculative fiction... There are enough people inside and outside of SF fandom who think that he is an asshole, period. Regardless, he does make valid points.

LeGuin is much softer than Ellison on the subject, but that is in part an illusion. On the surface she mildly criticises SF fandom for being conservative on issues of literary quality and the desire to maintain the genre ghetto. Yet the subtext, in cool tones, states that there is a substantial segment of the SF fan population that strongly desires that the genre be nothing more than infantile escapism and resist any attempt to expand the potential of the genre. The genre ghetto is their "safe place"; the safety of voluntary committal to a mental institution. Sometimes one can be more biting in a quiet, clinical voice than that of a screaming fury.

Malzberg places more emphasis upon the genre itself, but when he does focus upon fandom he makes some similar comments to that of Ellison and LeGuin -- but without the anger or the clinical tone. Here we have angst and a small bit of self-loathing for participating in this incestuous environment; the cross-over between fans and writers and editors and publishers, the entire SF community. The juvenile emphasis in the genre and in the behaviour of fans, the deep conservatism, the middle class fear of the different and non-ordinary. At least in this portrait, the blame is shared.

As for the fans themselves; they may use multiple voices, but in the end, they say the same damn thing. They agree in part with Ellison, LeGuin, and Malzberg -- in part, because what they usually agree with is that these behaviours are to be found within X segment of fandom. Of course X segment will say these negative elements are only to be found in Y fandom, and so it goes... Taken from a wide, collective POV -- it can be said that fandom does agree with the above critique made by the writers.

Further exploration of SF fan history and other fan documents
available on the web provides more than ample evidence to support
the statement made above; that SF fans are indeed "self-inflated,
troglodytic, provincial, back-biting, cowardly assholes." The
evidence is very strong and thus I will accept it as such; while
the evidence could be made even stronger through the use of
quantitative content analysis and statistical software, I have no
desire to devote several hundred person hours to this task -
which would only confirm what I have already stated.

As for personal experience, it largely agrees with what has
already been said. I have observed this behaviour over the
years, I have at times participated in this behaviour as a fan -
or viewed it from the side-lines - and thus do firmly support the
title of this article; SF fandom is deserving of a thorough
tolchocking. Where I would like to place my emphasis is on the
self-inflated, passive-aggressive, superiority/inferiority
complex I have observed in fandom over the years.

At the core, these perceptions stretch back to the very early
days of fandom -- the period known as First to Third fandom (more
or less) -- the 1930's to early 1940's. I will not rehash was
has been done in personal historical accounts or enter into any
debate about the "numbered fandom" time periods[8]. My focus is on
one of the major SF fandom feuds from this time and the
repercussions it continues to have on the present.

First, some context... In the 1930's the dominant medium was
print which was a mass market while simultaneously distributing
to niche markets (niche marketing is not new). This was true in
particular for the magazine trade, especially for the pulp
magazines. Within the pulps there were magazines for every genre
and subgenre, from nurse romances to baseball fiction, to
railroad adventures, to naval battle fiction, to science fiction,
etc. Print fiction was the primary form of entertainment for the
populace. Yes, there was cinema and the theatre, but next to
radio, print fiction was the most inexpensive entertainment. The
pulp short fiction magazines being paramount in that regard; they
were viewed as cheap entertainment for the masses (and if you
were of the middle class, you wouldn't be caught dead reading one
of those magazines). The low status accorded to pulp fiction
both for the writers and for the readers is one historical
thread.

---

[8] This was all well before I was born and covers a period when my parents were
infants to about age eight or ten.

This was also the time of the Great Depression. For a large
segment of the population, the economy had failed and doubt was
now being cast upon capitalism itself. Alternatives such as
socialism and communism were being advocated by reasonable people
as was the brand new alternative of fascism. In the aftermath of
World War I and with the rupture to the economic system caused by
the Great Depression, many people perceived that the system had
broken and that only a massive overhaul would remedy the
situation. Radical ideals were no longer unthinkable and many
people thought that only by radical change could there be any
restoration to the civilised world. This is the second
historical thread.

The major fan feud... I am going to simplify things (as always
historical events are more complex than the popularised accounts
made of them) here in my discussion (fan historians can pick nits
later) as I have already dwelt more on this than I intended to.
The feud was over the purpose of science fiction; one group
viewed it as escapist genre fiction that (with hope) also
inspired an interest in science and technology among the reading
public, while the other group viewed science fiction as a social
movement that could save the world (or at least make it a better
place). In the initial struggles, the latter group appeared to
trounce the former; however, at the end of the day, the former
group won the feud. There are very few SF fans today that
believe that science fiction is (or should be) a social movement.

The perception of science fiction as being a potentially world-
changing pursuit through the act of writing and/or even just
reading within the genre gave rise to the notion that science
fiction was important. That science fiction could save the
world... Later on (not that much later) was added the view that
science fiction and science fiction fandom were superior to the
rest of us "mundanes"; fans are slans (A. E. van Vogt's super-
intelligent evolved humans from the novel Slan), and therefore,
more intelligent than non-fans. This is re-echoed in the fan
acronym FIAWOL (Fandom is a Way of Life). The counter-perception
is that science fiction is escapist genre fiction and a good
thing too; I just want to be entertained, don't try and bother me
with art and politics and all that. Science fiction is a craft,
no more and no less. This perception comes with a built in
subtext of inferiority or persecution mentality; don't kick me,
I'm already down. Don't laugh at me for reading John Goobly,
Colonial Agent #37 -- didn't Tolkien say it is our "duty to
escape..." Yes, he did. However, LeGuin also raised the

question, "From what is one escaping, and to what?" If your
escape is into the phoney, into a cartoon-like world, that is
only a wish fulfilment fantasy; you have escaped by locking
yourself away in a mental institution.

Between the two poles of this binary presentation we have the
usual continuum of variation between the extremes. Science
fiction is a marvellous genre, a genre that can speak to the
issues of our time and our accelerating technological pace of
changes the way no other genre can; when we actually take the
effort to do so. Otherwise, it is just another genre of fiction.
It is not important. And, neither is science fiction fandom.
Sorry (well not that sorry), but it isn't. These words may be
tough for those who have volunteered many person-months
organising conventions, editing newsletters, writing fanzines;
people who want to perceive that all this unpaid labour was for
something greater. They want to believe that science fiction and
science fiction fandom has some higher purpose. But wanting to
believe something doesn't make it an actuality; it really
doesn't. To use the other fan acronym FIJAGH (Fandom is Just a
God-damned Hobby), period. And science fiction is just a god-
damned genre.

Pissing on a Pile of Old Amazings:

...a modest column by Lester Rainsford

How outrageous does one have to be today to get reactions? Or does the whole thing have to be published on Facebook and Twitter?

Toothless, we are toothless punks, chomping the dentures and reminiscing about the uprisings of '48. While everyone shambles by intent on their iPhone.

Editor's Note: Lester would appreciate some feedback on his columns...

Flogging a Dead Trekkie: Typical Fans

Neil Jamieson-Williams

In issue #10 I attempted to define the various types that are in connexion with SF fandom. Much of what I said there I still agree with, though there was a gross misinterpretation on my part with an email from Taral - thus, my definition of traditional fans is way off. I'm going to take another shot at this...

Genre consumers: These individuals consume science fiction and fantasy content in a variety of mediums from print to television to gaming, etc. They also have an interest in science fiction and fantasy collectables. They may attend conventions like Comic Con or Sci-Fi Fan Expo. People within this group do not identify themselves as SF fans.

Fans: These individuals consume science fiction and fantasy content in a variety of mediums from print to television to gaming, etc. They also have an interest in science fiction and fantasy collectables. They regularly attend conventions like Comic Con or Sci-Fi Fan Expo. People within this group identify themselves as SF fans; the male foursome from The Big Bang Theory would fit in this category. While it is possible that this type of fan could show up to Ad Astra or even SFContario, it is unlikely that this will occur - though, it would be probable that they may attend a fan-run convention like Polaris. The boundary between genre consumers and fans is a blurred one. If the person appears to be a genre consumer but they self identify themselves as a fan; the, they are a fan.

Active Fans: These individuals consume science fiction and fantasy content in a variety of mediums from print to television to gaming, etc. They may also have an interest in science fiction and fantasy collectables. They may attend or they may regularly attend fan-run conventions like Polaris and Ad Astra --

they may also attend conventions like Comic Con or Sci-Fi Fan Expo. They may participate the organisation and running of fan-run conventions. They may participate in genre based online forums, newsgroups, Facebook pages, Twitter feeds, etc. They may participate in writing fan fiction, blogs, networking sites, and fanzines. They may create crafts, visual art forms, and performance art forms related to the genre. They may network and organise within the fan community. People within this group identify themselves as SF fans. Most fans who attend fan-run conventions are active fans. There are three major subtypes of active fan; literary fans, media fans, and artisan fans. Literary fans are those active fans that place an emphasis on print medium science fiction. Media fans are those active fans that place the emphasis upon electronic media science fiction. Artisan fans are those active fans that place an emphasis upon artisan aspects of science fiction (building models, art, crafts, costuming, filk, fanzines, etc.). These subtypes are not exclusive, but an active fan will make one of these subtypes primary.[9]

Traditional Fans: These are active fans who identify themselves as being members of a local geographically-bounded SF community and who may belong to a local or regional SF fan organisation/club. In the past - twenty years ago and earlier - traditional fans were fandom. SF fandom was focused around local and/or regional fan organisations; everything was local for the most part. Traditional fans acted as fonts of information and as gatekeepers.[10] And most BNFs (Big Name Fans) arose out of the ranks of traditional fandom. Thirty years ago one way one could launch themselves into BNFdom was to have the disposable income to be part of a continental/intercontinental SF fan telephone tree.[11] Fan created their own emic[12] ideal types of specific

---

[9] Just to clarify; I am primarily a literary fan (though only by a small margin), who is also a media fan, and an artisan fan. The bottom line is, which of these three takes priority in your identity as a science fiction fan?
[10] I do question the utility of the gatekeeper role, from my recollection it only served create "trufan" exclusiveness - we are real fans and you're not...
[11] Back twenty or more years ago, long distance telephone calls were expensive, most people didn't have access to the internet, and there was no texting. A telephone tree was the fastest method to relay information across the continent.
[12] From the native's point of view - in this case the SF fan.

regional fandoms - the concept of a "mid-West fan" has probably lost all meaning except for those fans forty years of age and older. Back in my late teens I was a member of three different local SF clubs. These organisations were the focal points for fan communication and networking (both practical and social).

The rise of the web has winnowed the numbers of fan clubs. There are few organisations that continue to exist as actual fan clubs that have regular meetings, etc.[13] Much of the local/regional fan activity moved online starting in the late 1990's and, although it has moved around on the internet (few use Yahoo groups anymore and almost everything has migrated tor Facebook, for now), online is where the majority of fan activity takes place. With the decline of local clubs/organisations; traditional fandom has also declined. The traditional fans do bemoan this, but that is the way the technology is being used in our society overall. This is no something specific to fandom. But yes, it has diminished the numbers of traditional fandom and reduced their role as gatekeepers. Nevertheless, traditional fans do still exist.

So, there are the basic types I will be working with - for now. Further refining will take place as part of dialogue with various fans and through the SF Fan Survey that I will be conducting. Regardless, it is a base foundation to begin categorising within. Comments and suggestions are, of course, welcome.

---

[13] I would hazard a speculation that almost all of the clubs that still survive have a major role in organising an annual convention that attracts at least 400 or more attendees.

Scribbling on the Bog Wall: Letters of Comment

Neil Jamieson-Williams

As I write this, there is only two LoCs this time around. My comments are, of course, in glorious pudmonkey.

1706-24 Eva Rd.
Etobicoke, ON
M9C 2B2

March 11, 2012

Dear Neil:

Thanks for issue 12 of Swill @ 30…another busy weekend. I finally got myself a daytime job, working at an advertising agency in Mississauga, so letters like this may be short. I'll find out the hard way, I guess, or just type faster.

Goose-Stepping Towards Tomorrow…I had wondered if science fiction was a substitute version of the US' Manifest Destiny; if we can't take the whole continent, we'll go out and conquer the stars. Given how there's the old stereotype of nerdy little fanboys living in their parents' basement (I dislike this old meme, but there is always a kernel of truth in the middle), perhaps the young SF reader liked the authoritarian aspect because he was used to being told what to do, but in mentally assuming the role of the lead character in the story, he was finally in charge, confident, and had others do what he told them to do, a refreshing and empowering change. I must wonder, as we age, and we're presumably in charge of our own lives in a way we couldn't have had when we were kids, we no longer long for that era of adventure to the stars, and SF loses its appeal, and we find something else to read to exercise our brains, like suspense/detective/crime fiction. Much of the fandom connected with this other genre came from SF fandom.

Well the nerdy little fanboys do exist – I have actually met and observed some... Your comments about the authoritarian stream in SF does work for the past when the genre was perceived as a "children's/young adult" genre; however, it fails to explain the past 40 years. I would agree that as I passed my twenties I did try some other genres of fiction, and I still do read outside of science fiction, but discovered that much of the other genre fiction (and all fiction is genre fiction) was just as formulaic as SF and often more so if your read an author's entire body of work. SF does have the expectation that it is going to be more inventive, even when the attempt fails. But, I definitely agree that any desire on the part of the SF genre consumer for authoritarian adventures of the sort I outlined in issue #12, is a retreat into the infantile...

Any issues of Swill left to get? Have you been able to reconstitute a full set of issues yet?

Just issues #1 and #2... Didn't you say that you thought you had a copy of issue #3?

I also wonder about modern SF's quality over its quantity. Have a look in any issue of Locus, there's simply too much to read, and much of it is probably not to any given reader's taste. That's why I tend to stick to SF from the eras I liked most, the 60s, 70 and 80s. Familiar names, stories I like, and it's easier to say I've read most of it, too.

There are books that I re-read from the past and I also read new works as well. I am currently re-reading some Malzberg which I first read at too young an age to appreciate much of the content.

There is some pride in knowledge, and being able to relay to others the experiences you've had in putting together conventions and other events. You 'd like to be able to do that, to help others as they stage cons, and send them to school so they have some warning of the problems to come. Because those newer fans are new, they probably don't know you've done all this before, and they may decide you don't know what you're talking about, or the best way to learn is to do and make all those mistakes themselves. Every generation of fans reinvents the square wheel. Roll your eyes, and let them learn, and perhaps you may have the perverse satisfaction of hearing them say, I wish I'd listened... We retired from convention management because we were tired, but also because we suspected that our experience was no longer relevant or usable. People's expectations of conventions change, their interests change, and hospitality laws change, too. Dealers now require contracts for tables; for me, your cheque was your reservation, here's what we intend to provide for you and the room, go have fun and sell out.

Hospitalty suite have limited amounts of alcohol if any, mostly because of changes in liquor licensing laws, and a select few who didn't like the idea of beer in a con suite, and reported it to the LLBO. Newer people will have newer, more relevant experiences, so it was time to go, to let others take charge and allow them to get and use their newer experience. People never thought we'd ever retire, and when we did, there was some level of resentment, how dare we just go? Saying no has become easy to say, but nothing says we can't volunteer here and there, or set up some events of our own. We just don't want to be on the convention committee any more.

All true. And yet, it was the same when we were the young ones -reinterpreting the SF convention for our generation and our interests. Sometimes we listened to the old guard and other times we re-invented square wheels. At the end of the day, the younger ones have to be given the freedom to run things their way, make their own mistakes, etc. If establishment fandom attempts to prevent this; the young ones will just go start their own conventions anyway.

The nostalgia of a past fannish era, even one I wasn't a part of myself, was part of fandom's charm when I first got into it. Its history added a dimension that many other hobbies don't have. Now that I've been around for 35 years, that history is that much more distant, and while there is still nostalgia connected with it, I am finding myself part of more recent history. Some have made the observation that fandom is dying, and the reason for that is that fandom, especially the fanzine fandom I am still enjoying is the most unwelcoming group I could ever meet. I find my respect for the senior group, supposedly at fanzine fandom's heart, is lessening all the time because they use the virtual distance of the Net to slag others and cast aspersions on others they suddenly don't like, and I've been the target more than once, never knowing what brought that on. More than once recently, I have been tempted to tell them all where to stick it, start my own fanzine, and distribute it to those I still like, and to Canadian fans to promote the hobby here. I find a change in direction bumps you out of a rut, and I may be in a rut now. Time will tell.

Fandom is not dying, it just continues to change. Traditional fandom is indeed dying due to technological change and different foci of social interaction within society as a whole - though it is quite probable that traditional fandom will not go extinct, but continue to survive within the habitable niches that larger urban centres provide. Fanzine fandom is in decline for a similar reason - the current preference for blogging - but, like traditional fandom, fanzine fandom will continue to persist. Once the novelty of blogging runs its course, fanzine fandom may experience resurgence - though I can never see it reaching the prominence again that it once held in the palaeodigital[14] era or earlier.

Why don't you publish your own fanzine???

That was a longer loc than I expected. Off it goes, many thanks, and we will see you at Ad Astra.

Yours, Lloyd Penney.

Talk with you at Ad Astra...

March 30, 2012
Kevin Atchison -- relayed via Lester Rainsford

"I had a chuckle going thru Swill and seeing some very old "Fanzines" that I thought had been "consigned to flames of woe" some time ago. It is good to see that some of the old enthusiasm refuses to die. Give my regards to Neil and may he keep up with the imaginative work. But it is no Reticulum!"

Hi Kevin,

Yes, I had thought Sirius was long lost, but there it was in the Swill archive in Lester's possession. No fanfic fanzines for me these days - just SWILL. Of course SWILL is no Reticulum. Nevertheless, I think that the old issues of Swill still stand up, but I am not too certain that the same could be said for Reticulum. Nevertheless, Reticulum was good for its time... Send me an email, sometime. Neil

R. G. Cameron
The Frenetic Fanac Review #1
SWILL # 12 - February 2012
Faned: Neil Jamieson-Williams
Available at http://swill.uldunemedia.ca

Long story short, SWILL used to be a rude and crude crudzine sticking pins in the somewhat overly inflated ego-balloons of fen

---

[14] Roughly from 1950 to 1995. The Lower Palaeodigital from 1950 to 1970, Middle Palaeodigital from 1971 to 1980, Upper Palaeodigital from 1981 to 1995. Digital era begins post 1995...

everywhere, or such was the intention circa 1981. Neil revived it
last year in the guise of same, but in actual fact it may be the
most important and significant SF zine published in Canada today,
for its purpose is to definitively define what fandom was and is
through discussion and research. A dry, academic exercise?
Academic for sure, for that's what Neil is these days, but not
dry, rather a juicy morsel saturated and dripping with the old
Swill spirit, albeit far more articulate and meaningful than it
was thirty years ago.

Again, thanks for the kind comments regarding SWILL. I do disagree with your statement that
SWILL "may be the most important and significant SF zine published in Canada today..." I do
not believe that I am alone here, either. Your fellow fan historians Messrs Taral and Spencer do
not appear to hold the same opinion regarding the revival of SWILL.

Of course, one has to get used to the 'Pudmonkey' font
replicating a manuscript produced by a typewriter with dirty
keys, but that is merely the price of admission.

Hey Graeme, didn't you read the LoC column from issue #12? Pudmonkey is now only used for
article titles and my comments in the LoC column... or do you also have a problem with VT
Corona?

Now having praised SWILL for dissecting fandom most gloriously,
naturally the current issue has very little to do with fandom,
and instead dwells on how the evolving world is turning out to
even worse than dystopian SF predicted.

Ah, rest assured, fandom has been dissected in this issue...

In his editorial, titled "Goose-stepping toward Tomorrow," Neil
writes:

"There is an unfortunate and strong authoritarian undercurrent
within science fiction.... Ursula K. LeGuin in her 1975 essay
"American SF and the Other" also touches on this theme as she
questions the preference for, "authoritarianism, the domination
of ignorant masses by a powerful elite...democracy is quite
forgotten. Military virtues are taken as ethical ones... It is a
perfect baboon patriarchy"... And I agree, the passion for
authoritarianism in SF is a retreat to pre-human primate social
organisation."

Neil then talks about the typical SF authoritarian setup, cuddly
father figure benevolent dictators ruling over featureless masses
for their own good, etc., etc. I personally am not so sure this
reflects right wing tendencies on the part of the authors so much

as laziness. It's a lot easier to concentrate on a few nifty characters and leave the rest of humanity in the background than it is to conjure up a radically novel society whose cultural mores and motivations are mind-bogglingly different from our own and unlike anything in human history to date.

Still, what are the implications of Neil's premise, why is it important to note? He proposes that the SF in question has proven distressingly prescient, that we are in fact moving towards such a future. He states:

"...since the end of the Cold War, authoritarianism has been on the rise within the Western democracies. Civil liberties have been eroded (for our own safety), social programmes gutted, the average wage continues to shrink, the middle class is in decline, while our politicians vote themselves substantial pay increases, and our corporate CEOs hire analysts to recommend that annual compensation is inadequate and must be increased, the right to strike and collective bargaining is being curtailed, and the financial sector was permitted (due to the relaxing of government regulation) to create the worst recession since the Great Depression and handed the taxpayer, i.e. the average citizen the bill. The current trends point toward a more authoritarian future, everywhere...."

I happen to believe he is correct.

That is because you are a perceptive individual...

On the positive side, our near future will eventually make the old dystopian SF look like Utopian SF, and as a result SF will regain its popularity as harmless escapist literature. Just goes to show, there's a silver lining in every cloud...

By the way, Neil is looking for copies of the three issues of his 1984 zine DAUGHTER OF SWILL, MOTHER OF SCUM, his own having been destroyed in a basement flood (I think). If anybody owns one or more of them, he'd appreciate scanned versions being emailed to him.

Thanks for the additional request, especially as any copies would probably be found amidst the collections of Vancouver and Pacific North-West fandom.

Unfortunately for us, his opinion of his 1975 zine SIRIUS SCIENCE FICTION is "I have re-read the issue and to be blunt, my content really does suck, end of story. The only excuse (albeit lame) that I can give is that at the time that Sirius #1 was published I was 16 years of age..."

Unfortunate, that is, in the sense he is reluctant to scan it and share it with us. Personally, I think it would be representative of the teenage fan mindset of that bygone era and consequently a most interesting blast from the past… To be clear, I don't subscribe to a desire to read only the 'good' zines, the 'quality' zines, the 'best' zines, and so on. I have a historian's perspective. I'm interested in ALL zines (in the SF genre) be they award-winning masterpieces or crudzines, beautiful works of art or hopeless messes.

As Harlan Ellison once said, "It take's just as much effort to write a bad novel as a good one."

And the same goes for fanzines. It's that inspired if inadequate effort by beginners I'm especially interested in. Besides, most of the famous fanzines of first fandom were churned out by eager teenagers, and what a load of crap, especially political crap and libelous infighting is to be found in the pages they wrote, yet many gems too, or at least the beginnings of a fine crystal garden.

In short, I don't care if SIRIUS SCIENCE FICTION sucks! I Wanna reads it!

Graeme, I do agree with you in part, but only in part. There are two other concerns other than my opinion that my content "sucked". Unlike issues #1 and #2 of Swill, there is only one surviving copy of Sirius #1. To scan Swill #1 & #2 I had to remove the binding (not a big problem as it was a single corner staple). For Sirius #1 which had card stock covers, it was professionally triple stapled by the printer - while it can be taken apart, it cannot be returned to its original condition afterwards. The second concern is that this was a fanfic fanzine and that means that I do not have the rights to reproduce the fiction content that was written by others (fiction that the authors may wish to remain forgotten). What I may consider doing is retyping the non-fiction content that I wrote and my single story in the issue and making that available; but, only when I have the time to do so…

Anywho, check out last previous issues of SWILL which do indeed explore the nature of fandom

And congrats on yet another fanzine title - even though you are the CFFA grand pooh-bah, are you trying to insure a win of the CFFA by flooding the market?

Endnote: Survey Says...

Neil Jamieson-Williams

The first survey for the SF fandom research project is now up and running. This is not the only survey that will be conducted during the course of this project, just the first. As such it is a general demographic survey of fandom. I have chosen radio buttons for the survey and there is no option to choose "No Answer" for any of the questions asked. That is because I really need this exploratory data as the basis for the design of future surveys and formal interviews - plus it will provide the type of data required in the benighted hope that I may be able to obtain some SSHRC funding for this project. All responses to this survey will be anonymous and confidential.[15]

The survey is called SF Fan Survey #1 and it can be found at the link below

http://uldunemedia.ca/lime/index.php?sid=17227&lang=en

One final note about the back cover; there isn't one. Future issues may have a back cover, most will not. Although it has been a SWILL tradition to have back covers that trash a particular convention, not every issue of the old Swill did this. The tradition of detourned convention poster back covers will continue, but in a different format. I want to have the time to put in a good effort on this and to that end, I would like some input. Therefore, from now until November 1, 2012 there will be a poll running so that you, the fannish multitude, can select which Canadian convention should be honoured with having their convention poster detourned as the back cover of the annual issue (SWILL #17) that will

---

[15] Okay, if I really wanted to - and I don't want to - I could probably work out the IP address that you responded from. However, since most internet users today have a dynamic IP address assigned by their provider, this would be of little utility. Point is, it is for all intents and purposes anonymous.

be published February 2013. There are ten conventions on the list; the nominees are:

- Ad Astra 2012

- CanCon 2012

- Con*Cept 2012

- Hal-Con 2012

- Keycon 29

- Polaris 26

- Sci-Fi on the Rock 6

- SFContario 3

- VCON 37

- When Words Collide 2012

If there is a convention that you feel should be on the list and isn't you can email your suggestion to swill@uldunemedia.ca

The SWILL Poll is located here:

http://uldunemedia.ca/lime/index.php?sid=18567&lang=en

Till next time...

The **Pith Helmet and Propeller Beanie Tour**

April 2012 - July 2012

Ad Astra 2012

Polaris 26

SWILL

#14   Summer 2012

Table of Contents

SWILL is published quarterly (Spring, Summer, Autumn, and Winter) along with an annual every February - in other words, five times per year.

SWILL

Issue #14   Summer 2012

Copyright © 1981 - 2012 VileFen Press

a division of Klatha Entertainment an Uldune Media company

swill.uldunemedia.ca

Editorial: Big Ideas...

Neil Jamieson-Williams

Back in May, Lester sent me the link to a blog article, "SF, big ideas, ideology: what is to be done?", written by Charlie Stross.[1] This led me to the Neal Stephanson article, "Innovation Starvation".[2] Stephanson articulates that SF writers are "slacking off" and then discusses how technological (in particular the internet) and societal changes -- related to knowledge and risk -- have created "a system that celebrates short-term gains and tolerates stagnation, but condemns anything else as failure. In short, a world where big stuff can never get done." The Stross article is a reply to Stephanson and begins with examining the underlying assumptions; the Enlightenment concept of progress and whether or not "big ideas" ever really were primary to the genre. He goes on to say that in "recent decades SF has been spinning its wheels...(w)hat we call "hard SF" today mostly isn't hard, and isn't SF: it's fantasy with nanotech replicators instead of pixie dust and spaceships instead of dragons...(that we are) mistaking Sense of Wonder for Innovation." And wrapping it all up, Stross comments that we live in, but he doesn't use this term, a science-fictional world and that "(we) people of the SF-reading ghetto have stumbled blinking into the future, and our dirty little secret is that we don't much like it...(opening) the pages of a modern near-future SF novel now invites a neck-chillingly cold draft of wind from the world we're trying to escape, rather than a warm narcotic vision of a better place and time."

Any amount of whining about the lack of big visionary ideas about the future in SF really comes down to the whiner wanting escapism; where the concept (and the consequences) of progress are accepted as a default setting and never (or at least rarely) questioned. However, there is a lot to be questioned here. It was during the Enlightenment that industrialisation began in England and thus the foundations were laid for our current world with all of its benefits and its troubles. The philosophical concept of progress and improvement did not cause

---

[1] http://www.antipope.org/charlie/blog-static/2012/05/sf-big-ideas-ideology-what-is-.html#more
[2] http://www.worldpolicy.org/journal/fall2011/innovation-starvation

industrialisation (though they did offer fertile ground for industrialisation to take root in) and were it not for unique religious and political situation[3] that existed in 1660's England, industrialisation -- at this time -- may not have happened at all, yet (or have happened elsewhere and differently). During the Enlightenment, the notion of progress, while optimistic, was not automatic and the primary emphasis was upon societal advancement in all areas -- including science and the technological arts. It is a forward-looking philosophy and one that held out the belief that tomorrow would be better. And well before there was an established genre of scientific romances, the entire Enlightenment idea of progress was being challenged by the Romantic movement; in the end the Romantics lost and the Enlightenment ideals were transformed into rationalism and positivism (which were seen at the time as a more logical restatement of Enlightenment ideas). When science fiction emerged in the United States, it owed more to rational positivism than it did to the Enlightenment. The notions of progress and improvement began to be questioned in the mid-1950's, loudly during the 1960's to mid-1970's, and continues to be questioned in the present day.

Questioning is not the same as opposing; though many who hold a rational positivist worldview in the SF community seem to behave as if any questioning of progress is an attack as well as a cry to return to simpler times. I am 100% in agreement with Messrs Stephanson and Stross; I don't want to go back to the Upper Palaeolithic -- which is exactly the level of technology we would have if this current global civilisation collapses. I will go further and state that overall science and technology has improved the lives of millions of people and is responsible for the general high standard of living we collectively enjoy (some,

---

[3] In particular, just coming out of a religious civil war; the losers (Free-Churchers such as Presbyterians, Unitarians, Puritans, Baptists, etc. in other words non-Church of England Protestant sects) had to sign a loyalty oath to the Crown and an oath that they would not attempt to disrupt the Church of England. While, the oath to the Crown was not a major hurdle for most Free-Churchers, they tended to hate the Church of England more than the Roman Catholic Church, and there was a significant segment of the Free-Churcher population that dissented from signing both oaths - thus earning them the name, Dissenters. The Dissenters were barred from owning agricultural land (how the wealthy made their money back in those days) and from any form of public office (House of Lords, House of Commons, senior civil service posts, minor civil service posts). They could own land for resource extraction, engage in trade and commerce, or get involved in that new thing called manufacturing; all of which were viewed as being ungentlemanly. Nevertheless, it was the Dissenters that began industrialisation in England.

far more than others, but, even the poorest people on the planet tend to live better than the poorest people before (industrialisation). Scientific and technological progress have made much of human life better than it was in the past; how we have used science and technology has also created us a shitload of problems, too.

However, there are areas within society and culture that have not advanced as swiftly as our technology and scientific knowledge; in particular our systems of governance and economics. There has been little shift power to "we the people" -- post-American Revolution, this over a few decades became just window-dressing; wealthy elites (most of whom earned their fortunes via inheritance) control the political process, not the people.

Advances in technology have not resulted in advances such as more direct democracy -- but, they should have in a truly democratic society. Instead these advances have been employed to more skilfully manipulate the populace while at the same time eroding their civil liberties. All current economic systems have a built-in default setting that there must be progress in the form of growth; all claim that it is possible to have unlimited growth in a closed system.[4] This is impossible. While it was easy to ignore this impossibility in the 19th Century and the first half of the 20th Century it has become increasingly difficult to rationally ignore today -- it is irrationally ignored via referring to the impossibility as an "externality" and thus outside of the variables to be considered in economic formulae.

So, while I know that we cannot and should not abandon our industrial technology, and that the problems created by the use of industrial technology will probably be solved by new technology, as has happened in the past. I question how we have decided to use our current technology, who made the decisions, based on what data, and for whose benefit? I also raise the question -- because in spite of what our politicians, economists, and owners tell us, the biosphere of Earth **is** a closed system --

---

[4] The formulae that allow for this are highly suspect. First, there is the source of the formulae - physics. These formulae were an attempt to patch up Classical Mechanics and deal with electricity and magnetism; essentially the precursor to Aether Theory which was shown to be unnecessary by Relativity Mechanics. So what happened in the 1830's is that the economists plagiarised these physical formulae, changed the variable names, and proclaimed that they had made economics scientific. So just as neither matter nor energy can be destroyed (just transformed from one to the other) one can never exhaust a resource and one can have unlimited growth in a closed system. These formulae remain the fundamental formulae in modern economics to the present day.

4

how far can we push (that is degrade, wipe out, pollute, etc.) the biological systems that we depend upon before they collapse? And how is this a long term benefit for the corporate balance sheet; if you wipe out most of your customer base, who are your going to sell to in the next quarter? Actually, that is a rhetorical question -- we already know from the financial sector that corporations no longer look ahead beyond the next quarter and many plan only as far ahead as the next month. I question what is going to happen with our increasing automation and robotics. The automation that we have already implemented was supposed to have brought us more leisure time and the four-day work week; instead, we have higher unemployment/underemployment and those working full-time are working longer hours than people did before automation. As the automation and robotics progress, perhaps the only jobs that cannot be automated will be those that require creativity -- and if we develop true artificial intelligence, even that may be given over to the machines. So, what do the people do? What happens to them? And if the Singularity boosters are right, what happens if I don't want to be an upload, a cyborg, a genetically re-engineered being, or a superhuman cyberintelligence? Is there any choice in the matter? According to More, the only choice will be to accept this new stage in evolution and join in or face extinction -- unmodified Homo sapiens sapiens will not be permitted to stick around by the myriad subspecies of Homo novus.

So there is a lot about progress that can be questioned. There is also the possibility that the Singularity boosters could be wrong. Maybe genetic engineering, nanotech replicators, and artificial intelligence are more difficult to develop. What if we reach a plateau technologically -- we have in the past -- where there is just one thing/or a particular group of things that is missing that are required to move to the next level. Sometimes this has required a change in our theories of how the universe operates; more often it has required a cultural and social change.

So, I definitely agree with Stross that the near future projections based upon extrapolation do not leave me with any warm fuzzies; they conjure up visions of the engines of the night and therefore are more frightening than enlightening. I also agree with Stross that the average SF reader does not want this type of SF story; this type of story would be labelled as "dystopian", "anti-science", "pessimistic", etc. And for these same reasons, may be also deemed "unpublishable". That said, if one of the possibilities that one can extrapolate from current

trends in science and technology, projects currently receiving
R&D funding, is that in fifty years time we, the human species,
may have created our successors -- transhumans; how can one place
a positive spin on extinction? I also concur with Stross that it
is only a matter of time before mainstream fiction begins to deal
with the everyday angst associated with rapidly changing
technology and further invades the domain of near-future SF; with
the strong possibility of conquering this realm. What does that
leave SF with; escapism.

Perhaps one of the reasons why there is so much space opera,
alternate history, steam punk, etc. is to avoid having to deal
with the near-future. Face it, the near-future is difficult. By
2062 we will have already set the stage for a handful of possible
worlds; collapse (we blow this global civilisation and it has
collapsed or is in the process of collapsing), fortress states
(our elites lock themselves away in very, very large, nuclear
weapon defended, gated communities with all the goodies that high
technology will buy and the rest of us make it as best we can on
the outside), the Singularity (in one or more of its many forms,
thus an end, from our perspective, of humanity), post-scarcity
(with advances in nanotechnology, genetic engineering, automation
that are far more powerful that today's technologies but which
fall short of the Singularity that allow us to create a truly
post-industrial, post-scarcity civilisation), and variations on
these themes. On top of all that is the increasing pace of
change; how do you keep up and not be dated within a year of
publication? It is far easier to ignore the near-future (the
next 125 years) and set your story in the medium-future (126 to
300 years from now) or the far-future (over 300 years from now)
or within an alternate timeline. And that is what writers are
doing, many of them. And that is what the audience chooses to
read.

Stross states, "(W)e will not inspire anyone with grand visions
of a viable future through the medium of escapism." I agree.
That means that "big ideas" within the majority of science
fiction will be found on the margins of the genre, and they will
also be a minority.

Thrashing Trufen: Cri de Coeur

Neil Jamieson-Williams

Over the past year and a half I have heard an impassioned outcry
over the demise of fandom, in particular, "traditional fandom".
Of course, not everybody agrees as to the definition of a fan or
a traditional fan. And, as with most emotional appeals, there is
an underlying tone of protest or loss -- as what has happened is
in a way a paradigm shift and those howling are resisting and
fearing the perceived disintegration of identity and power. Is
this perception valid? Actually, it is. Will raging, whining,
and sulking restore things to the way they were? Absolutely not.

During the past eighteen months I have attempted to construct
working definitions of fandom -- as part of my research project -
- with limited success. Part of the problem has been bias and
the inertia of the past. Even though I have the rep of being an
arch anti-fan in the early 1980s, I was a fan. Back then, I
would have fallen into both my categories of active fan and
traditional fan. I engaged in a wide variety of fan activity
from writing and publishing fanzines to convention organising.
While living in Vancouver, I was definitely a traditional fan;
integrated into the local fan community which served as my
primary social network. So, I have come to this research project
with some outmoded concepts about what fandom is and should be;
concepts that I probably share with many people who have been
involved in the SF fandom community who are age thirty-five and
older.

In the old days -- I am not calling them "good old days", just
the old days -- in particular, the 1980's, things were different.
(Those under thirty-five who may be reading this, bear with me a
moment...) SF fandom has always been a subculture and as such
retains a strong connexion to the mainstream/dominant culture;
i.e. it bears a lot in common with the dominant culture. It most
certainly is shaped by the technology and the economics of that
dominant culture of any particular time period. In 1980, postage
was inexpensive, the average minimum wage was $3.50 per hour, it
cost an average of $1.15 per minute to call from Toronto to
Vancouver, only 20% of households owned a VCR, personal stereos
where still a new thing and used cassette tapes, if you were one
of the few who owned a mobile phone it was probably a car phone,

hardly anybody owned a personal computer, there were few BBSs around, and if you were connected to the internet it was only text-based. The technology and the economics of the time still encouraged local face-to-face social groups and that was the same for science fiction fandom. Local SF clubs provided a social network, local conventions also served this purpose, and if you lived in a city large enough to host a regional convention that convention would serve as a network with fans outside of your city. Fanzines printed via mimeograph and sent by post were another medium of communication within fandom. Thus, this was a time period in which the active fan and traditional fan thrived.

However, as I tell my students, technology changes everything.[5]

The technological context that was the environment of the active and traditional fan has been overshadowed by technological change. Mobile phones, tablets, the internet, voip, inexpensive long distance rates, online social networking, etc. have transformed society and culture. Like it or not, this is the way things are in the second decade of the 21st Century. Everyone under sixty years of age is a digital citizen to some degree -- and even most people between sixty and seventy five at least have email -- the younger you are, the more digital you are. If you are under thirty, you use social networking and text for most of your interactions; when you meet face-to-face that site was arranged via digital interaction. Community has become more ephemeral, more of an electronic haze of digital interaction than physical, limited to geographic space. That's just the way things are now and that impacts upon fandom. That is why only a few people will read this article -- it is published in a fanzine, albeit an online fanzine -- and fanzines are so 20th Century to the younger crowd (static, with no immediate ability to post comments). Fanzines, SF clubs, large fan-run conventions are the flotsam of cultural lag from the last quarter of the last century. The younger fans are not looking for an old-style local fan community; they have the community that they want via social networking and can arrange face-to-face meetings via that same networking software. When they attend conventions, it would appear that, they want high profile names as guests (be they writers, artists, actors, etc.), talks given by people who actually were involved in the cultural artefact (be it a novel, an online magazine, film, television series, graphic novel, etc.)

---

[5] I teach five different versions of the course **Technology and Society** at McMaster and Mohawk - the course examines the impact of technology on society and vice versa.

not just somebody that has an opinion on it (you can find tonnes
of that stuff on the internet), signing opportunities, a very
good dealers room, and hands-on workshops. In other words they
want the stuff, the experience, which they cannot get online.
And the social aspect of a convention is secondary at best,
possibly even tertiary...

To older fans, the younger fans can appear to be no different
than a genre consumer. This is an error, though an easy one to
make. Now it has been a traditional SWILL policy to defend the
genre consumer vs the typical SF fan; it will now be SWILL policy
to defend the typical fan of today, 2012. Not to make an
impassioned plea advocating this group, only to firmly and
decisively state that this is what fandom is now, period.

With that in mind, here are my revised categories:

Genre consumers: These individuals consume science fiction and
fantasy content in a variety of mediums from print to television
to gaming, etc. They also have an interest in science fiction
and fantasy collectables. They may attend conventions like Comic
Con or Sci-Fi Fan Expo. People within this group do not identify
themselves as SF fans.

Fans: These individuals consume science fiction and fantasy
content in a variety of mediums from print to television to
gaming, etc. They also have an interest in science fiction and
fantasy collectables. They regularly attend conventions like
Comic Con or Sci-Fi Fan Expo. They may occasionally attend large
fan-run conventions like Ad Astra or Polaris. They engage in fan
activity... They may participate in genre based online forums,
newsgroups, Facebook pages, Twitter feeds, etc. They may
participate in writing fan fiction, blogs, networking sites, etc.
They may create crafts, visual art forms, and performance art
forms related to the genre. They may network online and organise
within the fan community. People within this group identify
themselves as SF fans. Fan activity is on a continuum for fans;
some are more active than others, some of their fanac is more
visible than others. For those fans with low fanac, the boundary
between genre consumers and fans is a blurred one. If the person
appears to be a genre consumer but they self identify themselves
as a fan; then, they are a fan.

Traditional Fans: These individuals consume science fiction and
fantasy content in a variety of mediums from print to television
to gaming, etc. They may also have an interest in science

fiction and fantasy collectables. They may attend or they may regularly attend fan-run conventions like Polaris and Ad Astra -- they may also attend conventions like Comic Con or Sci-Fi Fan Expo. They may participate the organisation and running of fan-run conventions. They may participate in genre based online forums, newsgroups, Facebook pages, Twitter feeds, etc. They may participate in writing fan fiction, fanzines, networking sites, and blogs. They may create crafts, visual art forms, and performance art forms related to the genre. They may network and organise within the fan community. They may identify themselves as being members of a local geographically-bounded SF community and who may belong to a local or regional SF fan organisation/club. People within this group tend to strongly identify themselves as SF fans. Most fans who attend fan-run conventions are traditional fans.

Let the screaming and gnashing of teeth, begin.

Pissing on a Pile of Old Amazings

...a modest column by Lester Rainsford

This spring british writer Christopher Priest produced a little rant that gained some internet buzz. He felt that pretty much all the nhominees for the Clarke prize were basically suck and enumerated how they suck. Amongst others, amd most memorable, he chastized Charlie Storss as an 'internet puppy'.

Mr Priest - and I do ~~expect~~ hope that he called his sons 'Zadok' and 'Judas' - is wrong. On two counts.

First, sf needs internet puppies. Take Lester's internet puppies challenge: find a copy of the original Science Fiction Hall of Fame, in all its disintegrating Avon paperback ~~form~~ glory. Read it. Marvle at the internet puppieness of all those preinternet writers. They were having FUN. Does Mr Christ Priest not expect sf to be FUN? Maybe not. Too bad for him, too bad for readers who have FUN neither. (And leGuin's "Winds Twelve Quarters' came out more than thirty years ago. Good luck beating that. Don't bother.)

Second, Charlie is not really the internet puppie that he wishes he was, or that Priest preaches he is. I did read the five-volume Merchant Princes series. At the end is a jaw-dropping scenario that I won't give away. It would have been a great saw-dropping scenario in a short story, but to read a bzillion words over five books it was a "this sucks" moment for me. If you're going to end with an unbelievable jaw-dropping scenario, don't waste the readers time by making them read five books, just tag it onto a short story and be done. (Anyway if Zwelazny coulnd't rewrite the original Amber books into a second series, Storss doen'st have a hope in hell of managing it either. ~~Hint: Brand did it.~~)

A.E.Van VOgt. That's what sf needs, not Priests nor Strosses. Look, the universe is made up mostly of dark energy which the pyysisicsts know nothing about, expet that it seems to be determinging the fate of the universe. Oh yeah there's dark matter besides. And planets....planets MOVE. Ice planets migrate inward to become water worlds, and jupiters move into two-day orbits around their red dwarf suns. And who is writing about this stuff, stuff so new that physicists haven't figured it out yet?

I'll tell you, van Vogt would be writing far-out stories where the hero determines the pirinciples behind dark matter and uses it to defeat the evil floombs who are intent on moving Juipter within Mercury's orbit thus ~~rule sevagram~~ ejecting Earth from the solar system.

The crazy thing is that Van Bogt's wiritng wasn't that wild-ass far-out when it was written. Well~~, maybe it was. But~~. NO ONE KNOWS DICK ABOUT DARK MATTER AND ENERGY. SO THEY CAN"T SAY YOU"RE WORNG!!! So go wild. Use some imagination. And keep it SHORT. (Vogt's 900□-word scenes. Plot singularities. Space Nazis introduces from nowhere.)

Internet puppies of the modern scientific age. That's what SF need more of. Wjere is it? Come on! Kibble!!

Flogging a Dead Trekkie: Death of a Convention

Neil Jamieson-Williams

After 26 years, the largest fan-run media convention -- Polaris (formerly Toronto Trek) -- is dead. I never attended the convention in its heyday as I was 100% gafiated and if I was going to show up at a convention, during that time period (and I did attend Ad Astra 2001 for one day) it would be a literary SF con rather than a media SF con. I did attend Polaris in 2011 and 2012; there was a gallows tone to Polaris 26 as the organisation that hosts the event, TCON Promotional Society, had already informed those on their email mailing list that the end was neigh. In 2013, there will be a final Polaris 27, but this convention will be a ~~wake~~ relaxicon.

What happened? According to the TCON Promotional Society, "There are now a multitude of events going on all year, with traditional fan conventions being joined by Comicons and toy shows and autograph shows and pubnights and concerts and charity events of various kinds - there is now a fandom event of some kind in the area on almost every week of the year, especially in the summer months." This is indeed true. However, there have been times in the past when Toronto has been crowded with SF fan events that have made it challenging for large fan-run conventions. They have survived and come through this period of competition. What is different now?

One of the major issues is that a fan-run convention requires more lead time than that of a trade show event such as Wizard World or Fan Expo. Trade show events require the booking of a convention centre or large exhibition hall for their event; the event is more commercial than social and can be put together in a three month time-frame. A traditional fan-run convention has a more social emphasis; there are dealers but that is not the main focus of the event. This means booking function space within a large hotel and more advance planning. Because trade show events can be booked and organised in a shorter time frame and are put on by full time organisers (as opposed to fan volunteers) you can end up with the problem that faced Ad Astra this year when the Wizard World Toronto Comic Con was held on the same weekend. In the past, many of the trade show SF conventions were held by small companies operating either in Ontario or within the region. One miss-step, such as setting the date too close to that of a large fan-run convention, could bankrupt the company organising the event. In addition, given the small scale of the companies putting on these SF conventions, they would be able to bring in only the same calibre of names as the large fan-run conventions. This has changed. The corporations that hold the Wizard World and Hobby Star Marketing are large corporations, and Wizard World is a US corporation -- therefore, unlikely to give a shit about date conflicts with any Canadian fan-run conventions.

The other, as mentioned to me by one of my old droogs, is that traditional fan-run conventions are out of date; they are being organised by and for traditional fans -- which, as I stated in "Cri de Coeur", are no longer the typical SF fan. Thus, traditional fan-run conventions are targeting an aging and declining market share. This is not a major issue if you are running a convention like SFContario -- a general SF con with a literary emphasis -- that is aimed at the traditional fan and intended to be small; under 500 people. This is aimed at a niche market and so far the convention has been successful. However, if you are running a "big tent" convention like Ad Astra or Polaris, there are going to be problems in capturing the audience you need to bring in if your event only appeals to traditional fans. This only works when the situation is as "...(o)nce upon a time, there were only a couple of events for our core audience to look forward to every year"(TCON Promotional Society). Those under thirty-five will put up with (i.e. ignore) what they view as lame content if this is the only source for the content that they do want; you have a lot of latitude when you are the only game in town. It doesn't work in the face of competition that is providing the younger generations of the new typical fans with the content that they desire.

So, what's it going to be then, eh? Hell if I know... Okay, I
have organised and run over thirty special events, since my days
as a fan. None of these events had anything to do with science
fiction and nothing to do with fandom. So, while I know a fair
bit about running one to three day events; I don't really have my
finger on the pulse of Toronto fandom. I can say that in this
current environment that the way that things have always been
done is not going to work if you are hoping to/require to break
even a large number of attendees. The options are specialise,
downsize, integrate/work with the competition, or change so that
you can outcompete the competition. And I really don't see the
fan-run conventions being able to compete with the corporate SF
trade shows -- Anime North is only able to do this because it is
already specialised.

As for TCON's notion of hosting a big Doctor Who convention in
November of 2013 as the replacement for Polaris. I don't know
how that will work. [shrug] We'll all just have to wait and see…

Scribbling on the Bog Wall
Letters of Comment

Neil Jamieson-Williams

As I write this, there is only two LoCs this time around. My comments are, of course, in glorious pudmonkey.

Subject: Re: SWILL #13
From: "Taral Wayne" Taral@teksavvy.com
Date: Tue, April 17, 2012 7:38 am
To: swill@uldunemedia.ca

Canadian fans pay little attention to what goes on beyond their group in their city. Canadian fandom is particularly splintered and isolated. There is almost no networking between city fan groups and even within cities the fans tend to keep to their own.

Splintered is such a loaded term - reminds me of Trotskyites of the early 1980s. Fragmented is less loaded. Was Canadian fandom always fragmented? Possibly... Vancouver fandom in the 1980s was fairly unified; there were groups other than BCSFA but they really weren't warring factions. I would let other Canadian fan historians weigh in here. I think that Toronto fandom was always fragmented. Funny, I recall there being a fair bit of networking between cities; that s one of the things that BNFs did, back then (and had the massive telephone bills to prove it - unless they were/knew a phone phreak). I would hazard the speculation that there is even more informal and unofficial networking that goes on between cities today, but it is being done directly by fans themselves not via BNF spokepersons.

1706-24 Eva Rd.
Etobicoke, ON
M9C 2B2

May 4, 2012

Dear Neil:

I will pass on what seems to be the traditional greeting for this day, but I will say many thanks for the copy of Swill @ 30 13 you handed me at Ad Astra. Comments are coming...

Most of us are approaching 'old fart' status, and some have gotten there ahead of us. We remember what it was like, and regret that it's not that way now. We remember the good and the bad, and we've painted over some of the bad with the benefit of memory and its distance on our personal timelines. Overall, the good was great, and the bad didn't really hurt anything but our pride. We took some pride in our activities, and we sometimes felt we had some standing in our communities, and perhaps we had too much pride. It wouldn't matter if it was SF fandom or any other interest that forms a sub-culture around it, we'd find a place for ourselves within the community, and perhaps show a little too much pride. SF fandom isn't nearly as unique as it likes to think it, and the people within it are not slannish, but all too human.

Hi Lloyd... take a peek at my article "Cri de Coeur".

Too many people I know who do read SF do not take note of the themes within the literature, or enjoy the stories themselves, but who would prefer to lionize the authors, the same way media fans lionize the actors who portray their favorite characters. Many authors are troubled by this, and some just love the attention. The fragmentation of fandom into literary and media has always been unfortunate, and one of the factors may be attention span, whether you are willing to wait until the end of a novel or the end of an hour to get the story you want. It is also due to subjective desires, for some people I might have written off as mere media fans actually do have extensive SF book libraries, and a pile of DVDs; they just prefer the small and big screens to the book. We also want SF to be the literature others say it is not, and we've been haughty in its defence; this also chases people away to the less serious concern of enjoying any of the popular TV shows.

I think that most of the traditional fans cross back and forth quite easily between literary and media SF; except for the faans who have always been and always will be, fortunately, a minority.

It is perhaps the fact we have created a sub-culture centered around our enjoyment of science fiction that pushes it closer to popular culture, and away from literary culture. The fact the press has gotten their hands on SF and (their words) the geek and nerd factions doesn't help, either.

Literature is popular culture too. The genre of literary fiction tends to perceive itself as having no connexion with popular culture and that it is "high culture". As stated in the previous issue, I dont buy into that self assessment.

That radio play you mention...ever get it produced and performed? That's one kind of work I do pursue, voicework for any kinds of radio plays, usually student-produced.

I am assuming you are asking about "Only Fools and Knaves" ... I wrote and produced it back in 2001 using non-ACTRA talent and non-union director. So I am an evil, unfair engager and all that... ACTRA hadn't revised their radio agreement in almost a decade back then; they have since, but it is still written with the idea that the production company is the CBC. They need to take a page from Equity and have some sort of sliding scale based on size of house (in this case size of production company and access to distribution). I have been updating and re-writing the old scripts and then novella-ising them. I am also scripting a graphic novel. I do intend to attempt to produce the new radio scripts, but not until next summer at the earliest.

I have been on several e-mail groups that propose that the people within are the True Fans, the Secret Masters. I admit I aspired to be in the centre of things when it came to fandom, for I always enjoyed myself more when I was immersed in an activity. Now, I am pleased to sit back, relax a little, do what I'd like and not worry about any street cred I might blow by doing something a particular group doesn't approve of. Like tht song says, you can't please everyone, so you've got to please yourself.

I agree...

Lester would like some reaction? Okay. Piss away, Lester, obviously you're not offending anyone, and getting a rise out your readers. Time to kick it up a notch, and say what you really think. Modern fandom doesn't know what happened in '48, and those who do know and care are more and more a rapidly shrinking minority in their 60s, 70s and 80s.

Lester has informed me to say, "Thank you for supplying your address. A response will arrive in time, toadspawn.

I have the book on the history of science fiction fandom, and they could be written because the foci of fandom at that time were SF books, SF magazine, SF fanzines and SF fans themselves. Now, there is no single main fandom, in spite of what the sercon True Fen think, and that has reduced the community aspect of fandom, but certainly not eliminated it. Fandom does have a more modern history, but the only way to quantify it is by city or country or interest.

Sercon Trufen tend to be cranky Boring Old Bastards/Bitches who desire stasis. The community aspect has been reduced, but it hasn't disappeared.

Categories of fans…I'd be most comfortable in the Traditional Fan category. My own preferences are to be constructive and creative, and to relay information, for that is the true currency of fandom, to pass along con listings or information about deadlines or special events in the works. That is the truly positive part of fandom, that and the community that fandom creates.

Ah, I have revised them yet again. Feedback please…

My letter…that ad agency job ended prematurely, so the job hunt is on once more. I couldn't find any issues of Swill in my collection, so I need to take the time to look again. You are correct that every fannish generation has to learn somehow, and when I was a newbie, I had to learn too, or figure it out for myself. So many fail to remember their own neo days; remembering mine was the incentive to retire from the concom. We could all easily sit around a table and chat away about our own fannish histories and reminisce and laugh our heads off…unfortunately, that sounds more like a retirement home. WE still have things we want to do, and we are trying our best to make new friends of the new fans on the scene, and for the most part, we've been successful.

I've taken part in the SF Fan Survey #1...I shall remind Yvonne of it and see if she'd like to take part in it, too. The deadline is in July.

Thanks, unfortunately the response has been low and only two responses from Polaris 26... A new survey will be out in time for SFContario.

This is more of a letter of comment than I'd intended, but a good zine gets the writing juices flowing, I guess. Many thanks for it, and I will keep looking for further issues. It's been a good exercise to look at fandom from a relatively objective viewpoint, see how silly we've been, but also see what the beneficial parts have been. See you next time.

Yours, Lloyd Penney.

Other than the costumes, SF fandom is really no more silly than your average open-mike regulars or little theatre groups. Most of the same positive and negative behaviours found in fandom also manifest themselves within other sub-cultures.

All the best,

Neil

Endnote: Starlost Memories

Neil Jamieson-Williams

THE STARLOST

At the 2012 Polaris convention there was a The Starlost Reunion
panel, with Robin Ward and Gay Rowan. This re-sparked my
interest in this programme which has been billed the "worst SF
television series of all time"; especially as Rowan and Ward
imparted a perception of events during the shooting of the series
that had not been heard elsewhere. Harlan Ellison and Ben Bova
have both told their version of events, in essay form and in
fiction and there are written comments by Douglas Trumbull and
Norman Klenman on the web. The written source material I shall
be using are: "Somehow, I Don't Think We're In Kansas, Toto",
"Phoenix Without Ashes" teleplay, novelisation of Phoenix Without
Ashes by Ellison and Bryant, graphic novel version of Phoenix
Without Ashes, "The Word" series bible for The Starlost, The
Starcrossed by Ben Bova, "The Starlost: a new perspective" by
Dennis Valdron, historical background/context material (e.g. when
the WGA-W 1973 strike began), and anecdotal material mined from
the internet. In addition, I have talked with two FX people who
worked on The Starlost (albeit in very junior positions) plus
there are the recent recollections by the actors. Taking all of
this together I am going to attempt some detective work and on
the balance of probabilities construct an account of what may
have happened in the production of The Starlost.

Bias check: I was age 14 when the series first aired. I liked
it for several reasons, the core concept was cool, there was some
interesting issues raised in the episodes, it was Canadian SF
(you had to look hard in the credits to see that it was a co-
production) and those positives overshadowed the many scientific
and continuity and logical errors -- though even at the time, I

found the last two episodes ("The Bees" and "Space Precinct") to be stupid. Anyway, I was 14 years old and I liked it. Yes, the effects and sets were bad but no worse than what I'd seen on Doctor Who on TVO. The other thing was that we lived in the burbs just north west of Toronto and we didn't have cable at the time (we would get that the following year); that meant that our channel selection was CBC, CBC French, CTV, TVO, and one independent from Hamilton. I knew from friends who either had an antenna tower or cable of some of the things I was missing on USA television, but I didn't feel at all deprived as my situation was fairly normal for the time period. What I am saying here is that at that time I was young and really only knew Canadian television.

Bias check: I have a strong appreciation for Harlan Ellison as the artist, i.e. for his fiction -- the vast majority of his work I have enjoyed and many will be looked back upon as masterpieces in 20th Century literature. I have an appreciation for Ellison as the essayist; however, he has a tendency to use a 20cm brush to spread his tar and often ignores nuances, specific data, and cultural context. That said, he is an essayist not an academic. Harlan Ellison the human being is fallible and flawed (like the vast majority of us). I have met him one and one half[6] times and our second meeting in 1984 was no more positive than that in 1975, actually it was worse. This was at Westercon in Portland, a SFWA member from Seattle who had really liked the second series of the radio serial that I had wrote and produced introduced us, saying that I was from Canada and wrote radio drama. Ellison looked me over and said, "Get out of my face, Nazi motherfucker!" and walked away. To which I turned to the person who introduced us and said, "Wow; he really is an asshole." And that was it.[7]

---

[6] The first meeting or half meeting was a FanFair 3 in Toronto in 1975. This was my first SF convention. I arrived at the convention wearing a Starlost t-shirt and was abducted during my first hour at the convention by some men in their twenties who carried me into a panel room and presented me to one of the panellists who went absolutely apeshit, screaming something like, "get it out of here now before I have it disembowelled." I was informed later that the guy who went nuts over The Starlost t-shirt was Harlan Ellison; which didn't make an sense to me at the time - I had already read some Ellison so I knew the name, what I didn't know was that Ellison had created The Starlost.
[7] Again, some context. In 1984, I was a punk; I would have had a short Mohawk, be wearing black combat boots, dark jeans, and in all probability a t-shirt for one of the Vancouver bands. While the Vancouver punk scene tended

I have no grudge with Ellison, period. I also don't worship the ground he walks on or consider every word that escapes his lips as near-divine wisdom. Nor do I agree with everything that he says. I am only relating this to establish context -- we anthropologists love context.

Bias check: I was born in and, for the first ten years of my life, raised in Montreal, Quebec and although I am an Anglo, I do have a residual Quebecer's worldview.

Onward...

In February 1973, Ellison had a meeting with Robert Kline at 20th Century-Fox about doing a mini-series with the BBC. I would tend to agree with Valdron that Kline already had a package partially put together; the project probably already had Keir Dullea attached to it and interest from the BBC (Dullea was living in the UK at the time and refused to work in USA and the original mini-series idea "The Fugitive/The Prisoner in space" would be a project that would have some appeal to the BBC then). It is also probable that Douglas Trumbull was also already attached to the project and that it had been pitched to the BBC with Ellison as the lead writer of the series (before Ellison was even contacted); which is why Kline wanted Ellison so badly. In this February meeting, Kline pitches "The Fugitive/The Prisoner in space" concept and Ellison balks and gets up to leave; Kline asks him, "What did you have in mind?" Ellison would pitch him The Starlost, a concept that he had origonally planned for audio (either as a drama or reading for LP record) and Kline loves it. Ellison makes a 10 minute cassette recording of his pitch for Kline.

---

toward the left of centre and libertarian socialism, the LA scene had a significant segment of Neo-Nazi punks - it is possible that Ellison viewed all punks as being Neo-Nazis. In addition, this may have been the same day that Ellison found out at the convention that some fan was selling t-shirts that were making fun of him and which he wasn't making any money off of - two things that historically would have pissed him off. So, perhaps Ellison was having a bad day and was suffering from the perception that all punks were Neo-Nazis; it provides some hypothetical rationale for his rude behaviour.

According to Ellison, nothing happens between February and May -- and from his POV, nothing does. But obviously things happened in the interim. The BBC doesn't like The Starlost concept because it is going to require a higher budget than the original concept (there is a major recession going on and the UK is hit by it far more severely than the USA), so they walk. Kline would have shopped it around in the USA -- thus the scientifically inaccurate promo material he put out -- but, had the snag that Dullea wouldn't work in the States. However, Dullea would work in Canada and that is how CTV enters into the picture and Toronto as the production site.

Sidebar: Nobody else has discussed the Canadian Television Network in any rational manner. Ellison, Bova, and Trumbell all have taken their turn at trashing the CTV, Canadian creative and production personnel, and Canada itself. Some of this is pure blinkered tunnel-vision that Americans don't quite understand that, in spite of our many similarities, Canada is a separate country -- our differences are indeed, different. So was the CTV. The CTV was a private network, like what the USA is used to, but not. The CTV then, was a co-operative, it was owned by the independent stations that formed the network; the keystone being CFTO in Toronto. Incidentally, Glen-Warren Productions was a sister company to CFTO. So this was no large top-down network, more of a bottom-up (with each member station in the co-op having their input) with CFTO having slightly more sway than the others. Not understanding that CTV did not operate the same as USA private networks would be another problem for The Starlost.

By the time that Kline has got all his ducks in a row -- it is now an American style 24 episode series, to be shot at Glen-Warren Productions in Toronto, and aired on NBC and CTV -- he has secured Dullea and Trumbull, all he needs is Ellison. However, by the time he contacts Ellison again, in May, to have him write the series bible, the Writers Guild of America-West is on strike. Not only is Ellison pro-union, he is on the WGA-W executive; of course, he is not going to write a word until the strike is over.

However, Kline needs not only the Ellison name, he needs a series bible and a script for the opening episode, and all he has is an illegal/semi-legal (definitely unethical) transcription of Ellison's recorded pitch. So, Kline panics. He goes through a series of unethical schemes to get Ellison to write the bible and the first episode, he even hires a non-union writer to scab a series bible -- none of this works. In the end, CTV and Glen-Warren get ACTRA (the Canadian equivalent of SAG and AFTRA, and back then also the WGA -- the Writers Guild of Canada separates from ACTRA in 1991) to designate the series a Canadian production. What this means is that as ACTRA is not on strike and the project is under ACTRA's jurisdiction that Ellison could now write for the series. Ellison doesn't like the new situation, but he writes the bible and the first episode. Ellison claims that Kline urged and forced CTV to work this out with ACTRA, I don't think so. I think this was a CTV/Glen-Warren solution to Kline's problem. I also think that had Kline brought the problem to CTV/Glen-Warren as soon as his second meeting with Ellison was done (after all, he knew he had a problem, the WGA-W was already on strike) the same solution would have been arrived at, earlier, and without Kline generating a whole truckload of bad will by all the unethical means he attempted to get Ellison to write. Ellison would still hate this, and still bitch about it, but legal manoeuvring is not the same as full out unethical behaviour.

However, there is now an additional problem. The scab bible has already gone to Toronto and resulted in set construction that is counter to what is in the real bible. There was also confusion among the series producers and writing staff. Now add the fact that Ellison doesn't want to go to Toronto and once he arrives is upset with the producers and the writers as they "knew nothing about science fiction". Except for the fact that few producers or writers in television in 1973 would have experience in science fiction series, unless they were from the UK. Even then, not all of the SF television series in the 1960's and early 1970's were good science fiction, even the ones from the UK (e.g. Object Z, Undermind, It's About Time, Land of the Giants, Counterstrike). And some of the series writers did have some background in television science fiction, but not SF as a literary genre. As series creator (and the original story editor for the series) Ellison actually had a responsibility to work with the writers and mould them into a writing team that would set the tone for the show. According to the FX people I talked with (and this is echoed in part by the actors as well as the Valdron article) neither Ellison nor Bova endeared themselves to the production and writing teams, or the principal actors; both behaving like "ugly Americans". And, they got Canadian nationalism thrown right back at them according to Bova; no in your face aggressiveness, but under your breathe comments and most probably attitude.[8] There is a bit more on this from Ellison, I think; but since I don't have that source at hand, I will leave it.[9] One thing is certain, Ellison was (by his own admission) unable (or unwilling) to work with the series writers.

And so the much maligned Norman Klenman was brought in to assist Ellison; the two men did not hit it off, to say the least. Here, Ellison has said more (publicly) than Klenman. Ellison's comments are vitriolic; Klenman is a hack, a nobody, somebody's crony, who "didn't understand this science fiction stuff". Klenman began his work in documentaries and then crossed over into drama; he had worked for the CBC, BBC, and USA network television; he had worked on two previous projects with William Davidson (the Producer for the series) but had been called in by Arthur Weinthall (Head of Production at CTV) to please be the story editor for the series. His task was to work with Ellison and the writers to develop the themes for the series, hire the writers, edit, polish, and rewrite; Klenman was also (it would appear for the subtext) to act as a buffer and/or (if at all possible) to handle Ellison. The two men ended up in an

---

[8] With the series being designated a Canadian production by ACTRA and Ellison and Bova trashing Canada, the City of Toronto, and everything else Canadian, I can easily see an attitude begin to emerge; this is a Canadian show, listen to the "white shoes" (CTV/Glen-Warren execs at the time all wore white dress shoes) and fuck the damn Yanks.

[9] I am on holiday right now and have no interest in going into my cubicle to check my first edition paperback copy of Phoenix Without Ashes, which has the original version of Ellison's essay "Somehow, I Don't Think We're In Kansas, Toto". The version in my copy of Stalking the Nightmare is different - I cannot find the quote I'm looking for and there are all these references to series such as *Battlestar Galactica* and *Buck Rogers in the 24th Century* and the movie *Star Wars*, which obviously were not in the version published in 1975.

adversarial relationship from their first phone call -- though, this would seem to be more due to Ellison than Klenman. Klenman also has negative words about Ellison, that Ellison is "explosive and acidic" and that the first draft of "Phoenix Without Ashes" was "boring, turgic, biblical, heavy, and dull". Klenman also states that Ellison was egocentric, vengeful, and infers that Ellison will do anything for money (provided his price is met).

Nearly forty years after the events in question, my interpretation based on the information available is this: because of the WGA-W strike and Kline's attempts to get Ellison to write during the strike, because of the scab bible (and possible other scab writing) sent to CTV by Kline, because of how this poisoned the relationship between Kline and Ellison, because these events there was a state of confusion at Glen-Warren/CTV when Ellison arrived; Ellison came to Toronto in not the best of moods -- he didn't take action to make anything better. On the part of CTV/Glen-Warren, they had received what they had been told was the series bible from Fox only to have that reversed when the real bible appeared. The arrival of the series creator did not ease confusion, only add to it. Ellison was uncompromising and also absentee -- his mother was ill and he also had previous speaking engagements to attend. In the end CTV brought in someone (Klenman) their people had worked with before (successfully) to be the story editor as the series creator didn't appear -- from their point of view -- to be interested in actually doing any story editing. Ellison interpreted this as a further betrayal by William Davidson, CTV, and Robert Kline. In a less hostile atmosphere, it is possible that Klenman and Ellison could have worked together, which would only have served to improve the series itself.

To further add to this toxic mix, the effects promised by Douglas Trumbull were not working. First, the Magicam system was not reliable and when it was, it didn't really work too well on videotape.[10] The Magicam system used two cameras, one filming the actors against a blue screen, the other shooting a model background. When operating properly the motion of both cameras

---

[10] Note: it was Ellison who insisted that videotape rather than film be used for the series.

would be synchronised and scaled -- which would allow both the camera and the actors to move through model sets. This technology had been a key factor for the series; it would permit massive savings in sets. The failure of the Magicam system[11] really hurt The Starlost, in lost time, expense in trying to get the system to work, the construction of models that couldn't be used effectively, and now having to build sets in studio space too small. Because so much of the budget had been spent trying to get the Magicam system to work, there was now a shoestring budget remaining for the sets -- and that definitely showed.

Other factors that impacted the series were: that Trumbull and Dullea were more experienced with cinema than with television; that Canadian television personnel had little experience with the 1 hour episodic drama format (Canadian television preferred the 30 minute episodic format or the 90 minute television movie); that SF as a genre is not as strong in Canada as in the USA and we Canadians have a tendency toward slipstream [12] (SF with ghosts, urban fantasy, new weird; and that, with the lack of focus from Ellison, the stories told had a more Canadian worldview than an American one. In the series bible there is a section "WHAT KINDS OF STORIES WOULD WE LIKE TO TELL"; many of the suggested ideas that Ellison places in this section, were developed into scripts for the series. However, not in the way that Ellison or Bova would have envisioned; I agree with Valdron, that these episodes (for good or bad) had Canadian undercurrents to them which would not resonate with USA audiences.

At the end of the day, there is no simple answer as to why The Starlost failed as a series -- there are multiple reasons. And there are multiple reasons why it almost succeeded; it did come close to surviving, even with NBC and Fox pulling out. If they had produced just four more episodes, there would have been a possibility that CTV may have renewed it for a second season. The ratings for the series in Canada were acceptable, not great, but acceptable. Was it the worst SF television series of all time? No, it was not -- the British-German co-production for the

---

[11] Trumbull would have success with the Magicam in 1975 and it would be used successfully until it was superseded by superior technology in 1983.
[12] We actually like this a lot as a culture, far more than the Americans do - recent examples are the series *Being Erica* and *Saving Hope*.

late 1970s *Star Maidens* is a far better candidate for that title.
Was it a missed opportunity? Yes, indeed.

The Pith Helmet and Propeller Beanie Tour

July 2012 - December 2012

SFContario 3

SwILL

#15   Autumn 2012

Table of Contents

SWILL is published quarterly (Spring, Summer, Autumn, and Winter) along with an annual every February - in other words, five times per year.

SWILL

Issue #15 Autumn 2012

Copyright © 1981 - 2012 VileFen Press

a division of Klatha Entertainment an Uldune Media company

swill.uldunemedia.ca

Editorial: Triumph of the SWILL

Neil Jamieson-Williams

*** We interrupt this zine to present this editorial in Pudmonkey ***

As you may have noticed on the front cover, SWILL recently received two fan awards given at VCON 37 in late September. While one award was expected, the other was a surprise.

The Elron Awards are fandom's longest running spoof awards -- awarded for the worst contributions to science fiction/science fiction fandom during the previous calendar year. The awards are presented annually by the British Columbia Science Fiction Association (BCSFA) at the VCON convention. Way back in 1983, I was nominated for an Elron award for "Worst Fanzine Editor". I didn't win and I don't know who did. Interestingly, the nomination was not for Swill, or for Daughter of Swill (which was published in 1983); it was for my one year tenure as editor of the clubzine BCSFAzine. Not everyone in the club enjoyed by editorial style to put it mildly. I brought a mild Swillesque attitude to the tame and tepid clubzine. There were Swill-like editorial rants, some Miriad-like (Miriad was the semi-prozine published by the other three droogs) droog material, and lots of filler material gleaned from the contemporary punk subculture of the time. In my defence, I did raise the production values on the zine, published it on time, included all the material that came from the club, and (memory is hazy on this one) but I recall actually moderating the LoC section of the zine -- keeping a lid on things rather than pouring petrol on the fire like other BCSFAzine editors. Not everyone liked what I did, hence the nomination.

In email with the current SMOE (Secret Master of the Elrons) I suggested that I be awarded an Elron for "Worst Fanzine Editor of all Time" or "Lifetime Achievement for Worst Fanzine Editor" at VCON 38 -- being 30 years after the original nomination. The SMOE suggested that SWILL win a "Worst Fanzine" award which would be awarded at VCON 36 last year, but secret master things intervened; nevertheless, I kind of expected that SWILL would win some sort of Elron this year, and it did. SWILL won "Worst Fanzine" for the use of the pudmonkey font.

2

What I didn't expect was to receive a Faned -- the Canadian Fanzine Fanac Award -- for "Best Fanzine". This is actually a bit of an honour as it means that at least some people out there like what I am doing, here. It makes a nice counterpoint to those out there who have commented that SWILL is not and never has been a fanzine and that I am not and never have been a fan.

Now, these comments are rooted in the context of those fen who subscribe to the worldview that only the traditional trufan faan is a real fan. Definitely, from this perspective I am not and never have been a fan. I have never been part of the trufan faan sub-subculture where faanishness is paramount, eclipsing the genre itself, and I never will. From my perspective, the genre is central and always will be. I am a fan of the science fiction genre, first and foremost. Am I a fan of fandom? That is a more difficult one to answer.

What I am not a fan of and never will be a fan of are the superior than thou, lord high arbitrator of fannishness, protector of the precious bodily fluids of trufandom, fughead trufan faans and their version of fandom. As for fandom in the larger perspective, I have no issues. Am I a part of it? I once was and now...I am marginally part of it. Yes, I have been pubbing SWILL, I have been attending conventions, I have been participating as a panellist/moderator, I have donated some of my time to convention volunteering; all of which could be viewed as fanac. However, as the traditional trufen faans have pointed out, this is all in connexion to my research project and thus cannot be counted as fanac; I am either a non-fan or an ex-fan who is researching fandom. I beg to differ. As a researcher, I didn't have to revive one of my old fanzines to use in part as a means of communicating the progress of the research project. As science fiction conventions are public events -- if you find out about it and pay your membership, you can attend -- I technically didn't even have to notify the organisers that I was studying the convention and those attending it (it is good form to do so, but ethically, it is not required for public events). I did not have to do any volunteering, sit on panels, etc. I chose to do this, because I asked myself the question; back when I was active in the fan community, as a fan, what approach would I like to see from a researcher? Maybe my answer is a dated one -- so be it. Am I currently a part of the SF fan community? Yes, but only marginally. Look even when I was heavily involved, I was more a FIJAGDH fan anyway; the hobby has simply moved down several strata over the past 30 years to being just a step above gafia.

Also, the traditional trufan faans have tarred me with the brush of crudzine -- as if that was a concern. Look losers, I knew how to put together a decent -- not killer, but decent -- layout back in the days of electric typewriters and electro stencil and mimeograph. Guess what, like everything else today, with the technology available in your average office productivity software, it is an even far simpler task to do so. It is not that I cannot do so; it is because this is a conscious, definite choice being made by moi, the editor of this zine. As was the choice of the pudmonkey font. For a moment, just a moment, over clock the atrophying grey matter in your skulls and consider the standard dictionary meanings for the word chosen as the title of this fanzine. This is still an old-school punk, pare-down-to-the-basics, content over form, in blessed text alone, zine being written by a middle-aged punk/academic/sf genre consumer-marginal fan that has a slightly gentler tone than 30 years ago due to the fact that the editor and columnist (Lester Rainsford) are no longer in our twenties. Do you traditional trufan faan fuckheads actually believe that I am going to give a shit that you call SWILL a crudzine?

SWILL is a crudzine by intent and design and proud of it. SWILL won the Elron for its crudzine aesthetics and yet, surprisingly, won the Faned for its stripped-down, no whitewashing content. Perhaps the traditional trufan faan gatekeepers might consider pondering this... But no, there are more serious matters to be dealt with, such as, why everyone in Third Fandom Transitional B were a bunch of assholes...

*** We now return to this zine in VT Corona, already in progress... ***

Thrashing Trufen

Fen, True and Otherwise

Neil Jamieson-Williams

Okay, here we go again...

Traditional Fans:
Also known as trufans, fanzine fans, and other names. I prefer
the term Traditional over fanzine fan -- not all fanzine fans are
Traditional fans. The term trufan is loaded and implies that
Traditional fans are the only real fans and that everyone else is
a fakefan. So, what is a Traditional Fan? In the context of the
present, a Traditional Fan is a faan; a person for whom science
fiction fandom is of primary and central importance,
overshadowing interest in the genre. Traditional Fans place
emphasis upon the older tropes and memes within the science
fiction fan subculture; tropes and memes that emerged prior to
the mid-1990s. Examples of this would be the primary importance
placed upon fanzines, the fannish exchange systems, clubs, and
regular face-to-face community. While fandom itself (usually
capitalised by Traditional Fans) is central, for most Traditional
Fans the genre itself continues to have importance, albeit
secondary or lower. Traditional Fans consume science fiction and
fantasy content in a variety of mediums from print to television
to gaming, etc. They may also have an interest in science
fiction and fantasy collectables. They may attend or they may
regularly attend fan-run conventions like Polaris and Ad Astra --
they may also attend conventions like Comic Con or Sci-Fi Fan
Expo. They may participate the organisation and running of fan-
run conventions. They may participate in genre based online
forums, newsgroups, Facebook pages, Twitter feeds, etc. They do
participate in writing fan fiction, LoCs, and fanzines. They may
create crafts, visual art forms, and performance art forms
related to the genre. They may network and organise within the
fan community. Traditional Fans often like to call themselves
trufans and do tend to view all other fans as fakefans or genre
consumers. Traditional Fans are a declining segment within the
science fiction fan subculture.

Active Fans:
In the context of the present, and Active Fan is someone who is not a Traditional Fan who has some level of fan activity within the science fiction fan community-at-large, i.e. not necessarily bounded to a distinct geographic fan community. While most Active Fans have multiple fan activities and often engage in those fan activities within a distinct fan community (e.g. Star Trek fan community in Toronto); one can be an Active Fan even if you have a single fan activity (drawing cartoons) that only appear in SF convention programme books. Active Fans tend to view themselves as being simply fans. Active Fans consume science fiction and fantasy content in a variety of mediums from print to television to gaming, etc. They may also have an interest in science fiction and fantasy collectables. They often attend or they may regularly attend fan-run conventions like Polaris and Ad Astra -- they may also attend conventions like Comic Con or Sci-Fi Fan Expo. They may participate the organisation and running of fan-run conventions. They may participate in genre based online forums, newsgroups, Facebook pages, Twitter feeds, etc. They may participate in writing fan fiction, fanzines, networking sites, and blogs. They may create crafts, visual art forms, and performance art forms related to the genre. They may network and organise within the fan community. For the Active Fan, the genre is central and fandom is secondary; though for many Active Fans the fan community remains important. Active Fans place an emphasis upon the tropes and memes that emerged within the science fiction fan subculture between (roughly) 1980s and 2004. As a segment within the science fiction fan community, Active Fans are beginning to decline in numbers.

Digital Fans:
This term is being used (borrowed from Arnie Katz) for lack of a better term. This term describes those people who self-identify themselves as fan but have little or no fan activity within the established fan community. For the Digital Fan, the genre is primary and established fandom is tertiary or lower. However, most Digital Fans engage in fan activity outside of the established fan community through social networking and other digital means. While they perceive themselves as fans, while they interact with other fans like themselves, they rarely interact within the established fan community. Digital Fans consume science fiction and fantasy content in a variety of mediums from print to television to gaming, etc. They may also have an interest in science fiction and fantasy collectables. They tend to attend trade show style conventions like Comic Con

or Sci-Fi Fan Expo and rarely ever attend fan-run conventions like Polaris and Ad Astra -- and if they do it is to see a particular guest or to go to the Dealer's Room. Their primary fan activities tend to be digital or digitally mediated; e.g. writing blogs, newsfeeds, fan fiction, and sometimes digital fanzines. This form of digital fan activity tends to run separate and parallel to that of established fandom. Like other fans, Digital Fans may create crafts, written/visual/performance art forms related to the genre. Fans of this type will often be viewed as being "mundanes" by both Traditional Fans and Active Fans, though Active Fans may exhibit more tolerance for the Digital Fan. Digital Fans place emphasis upon the tropes and memes that have emerged in the science fiction subculture since 1998 (roughly). Digital Fans are a growing segment of the science fiction fan community.

Genre Consumers:
These individuals consume science fiction and fantasy content in a variety of mediums from print to television to gaming, etc. They may also have an interest in science fiction and fantasy collectables. They are the major audience for conventions like Comic Con or Sci-Fi Fan Expo. People within this group do not identify themselves as SF fans. These persons would be viewed as "mundanes" by Traditional fans, Active Fans, and Digital Fans. While these people exist outside of the science fiction fan community, the majority are strong fans of the genre. It is from this population that the majority of the people who make up the science fiction fan community emerged from (while there are a few cases of individuals discovering fandom first and then the genre, for the majority, they discover the genre and then fandom). As the genre continues to grow, this population of genre consumers is doing the same.

So, what does this all mean? Well one thing it means is that Traditional Fans are are very small and shrinking segment of the science fiction fan population. It also means that Active Fans are a segment of the population that is aging and beginning to decline in numbers. Yet, Digital Fans and Genre Consumers are on the rise. That means that, as I have said before in this zine, fandom is in transition; that fandom is changing. The big question is what fandom is changing into; that has yet to be determined, all that is certain is that it will be a different fandom.

Pissing on a Pile of Old Amazings:

...a modest column by Lester Rainsford

I am pissing on a pile of old Amazings. The urine arcs, braking into blobs, shimmering. It splashes on the pile of pulps. The yellowed pages of the old magazines become yet yellower. Arc, shimmer, splash, yellow.

The sound is like bumblebees in summer. The drops, pulled together by surface tension, throw out rays of light like liqied amber. The yellowing stain on the Amazingas has the suspect sheen of ~~noantechnology~~ nanites gone bad. The drops freeze in their arcs, turning into merrygorounds with pinik ponies. The buzzing of bees intensifies into the roaring of a Saturn v on launch.

Sone of a bitch, it's a VR scene. And if there's anything Lester does not approve of in "today's" SF, it's vR. Becasue, well, the authoer can spin on this kind of crap for pages and pages while the story doesn't get anywhere. I cyould have gone on for pages, but The Swill would have dealt with me.! In slomo. Like a John Wu film. The bullet would slow down, we could see it spin as it ambles towards my forehead , then the entry would and worse yet the exit wound.

Why does VR devolve to either a HonkGong ganstger film slomo or into the writer's last RPG campaign? Damned if I know but it sucks.

To that end, I have recently read The Quantim Theif and at the end I was no more enlightende but a few hours older. In addition, all I can say of Revenge of the Ners is, would have made a great rasfw joke but really, there was no need for an entire book. No need at all. the vacuum of ideas in VR is obvious, because it gets replaced by stream of consciousness just like this colum.

Years ago Ze3lazny threw in all kinds of filler in the Amber series-the transitions between worlds. I skipped it. and you, reader, should skip today's vr storeis. You, and the Sf field, will be better for that.

Flogging a Dead Trekkie:

Triumph of the "Mundanes"

Neil Jamieson-Williams

I am going to restate something that appeared in Fanstuff #21 because I like it and because it is useful. It is what Arnie Katz calls The Epoch Theory of Fandom -- though I think that it would be better termed the Epoch Approach to Fandom/Fanhistory. This is looking at fandom through a wide-angle temporal lens. Katz's Epochs are:

"The Eo-Fandom Epoch (- 1932). Science fiction became a genre, individual fans contacted each other and local and national fan clubs appeared.

The Fanzine Epoch (1933-1973). The first fanzines appeared in the early 1930's and quickly became the focus of fan activity.

The Convention Epoch (1974-2004). Conventions proliferated exponentially in the 1960, which gave birth to a much larger Fandom in which con-going and conrunning assumed a central position in Fandom.

The Digital Epoch (2005-). Desktop publishing, the Internet and Social Media are in the spotlight today."

I would also add to this that the rise of Mass Fandom would appear to have taken place during the Convention Epoch and is a dominant factor in the Digital Epoch.

Katz's Epoch Approach overlaps, in my view, quite nicely with my classification of fandom. The Traditional Fan is a product of the Fanzine Epoch and those who still hold onto the dominant subcultural traits of this Epoch are the Traditional Fans of today. As the Convention Epoch grew dominant the subcultural traits that characterise the modern Active Fan emerge; I think

that fan-run conventions and the style of fandom practiced by
Active Fans go hand in hand. The explosion of what has been
called Mass Fandom was fuelled by the increasing acceptance of
the genre within the entertainment industry and the "big-tent"
approach (something for everyone) that started to become common
in the latter years of the Convention Epoch. The Digital Epoch,
I think, has less to do with desktop publishing and the Internet
(though both are important), and more to do with social media,
texting, and mobile technology. Most definitely the type of
fandom that I have classified as Digital Fans is fully at home in
this particular Epoch.

While the dominant form of fan activity persists into later
Epochs, they cease to be dominant. The dominant form of the
Digital Epoch has yet to be determined other than it will be
mediated by social media and mobile technology. We are still
only eight to 12 years into the transition. Nevertheless, the
shift has occurred and it is not going to go away. From the
fannish point of view of Traditional and Active Fans, Digital
Fans are most definitely not fannish; in that Digital Fans have
less interest in established fandom. They appear to be in the
process of creating their own version of a fan community, but a
fan community that is ever shifting and mutable -- for ever in
the now, and just as ephemeral as a moment. It is not the sort
of fan community that Traditional or Active Fans are used to. It
is not the type of fan community that has a strong traction in
the face-to-face physical world.

Tradition Fandom was rooted in physical community, regions, and
face-to-face meetings (local club meetings and socials, collating
parties, pub nights, etc.), where conventions were events you
attended so that you could actually meet face-to-face the fans
that you knew only through personal lettermail, LoCs, or the
telephone. Active Fandom retained that face-to-face aspect of
Tradition fans, but with less emphasis on the local community and
more emphasis on the local and regional convention circuit. In a
way, the conventions were the community; a community more bounded
in cyclical time that gathered together in one locale for a few
days before it dispersed to the winds, to re-form again in
another location on the convention circuit. Digital Fandom as a
community is like an electronic haze that manifests itself into

small face-to-face groups for a few hours before returning to an electron state. Only at events such as Sci-Fi Fan Expo or Comic Con does it materialise en mass, yet even then it remains in a state of flux.

Digital Fandom is different. Personally, I'm not certain if it is my type of fandom -- I feel more at home within the Active Fandom of the Convention Epoch -- but, regardless, I am not about to disparage Digital Fandom. While it may not be a type of fandom that I am comfortable with -- look I still prefer email and voice over text and Facebook -- but it is where fandom is going. You may like the trend; you may not. However, you cannot stop it. And it serves nobody to sit upon your self-appointed throne and decree that, "Thou art not fandom, thou art mundane." Seriously, it doesn't. At best, you get to preach to the converted (those who think just like you do) but it is not going to make Digital Fandom disappear. Not at all. Go ahead, call them all mundanes, for all the good that that will do. Consider this, Traditional Fandom is greying and shrinking fast; Active Fandom is aging and starting to decline in numbers and influence. Guess what type of fandom is attracting the young people? Guess what type of fandom is growing in numbers and influence? Guess what type of fandom is going to become dominant and triumph? At least until the next Epoch begins...

Scribbling on the Bog Wall
Letters of Comment

Neil Jamieson-Williams

As I write this, there is only a single LoC this time around. My comments are, of course, in glorious pudmonkey.

1706-24 Eva Rd.
Etobicoke, ON
M9C 2B2

September 12, 2012

Dear Neil:

Swill 14 has been sitting around and stewing the last few weeks…life gets in the way when you're trying to get things done. That's my explanation and I am sticking to it. Here are comments on this issue.

More and more, I am finding that modern SF, what little of it I read, just doesn't do it for me. Even a book like Among Others by Jo Walton, which won the Hugo and Nebula this year, I've started it, and am having trouble continuing with it. It's not the book, it's me. I think I'd rather read the galaxy-exploding stuff from the 60s and 70s. That's my own Golden Age. I've aged right out of current SF's demographic. Genetic engineering and nanotech are hard SF, but perhaps not as hard as those golden years' tech. Somehow, they seem just a little softer. Any future today may be difficult to deal with, given how negative our outlook may be. And, given that we live very much in an SFnal future today, can we imagine that our own SFnal future would look like?

*** Everybody has a "golden age"; mine would sort of correspond with yours temporally and then again not. The same time period, the 1960s and 1970s, had a definite influence upon my SF tastes. Some of what I read during that time period was old like Childhood's End and some was brand new such as Rendezvous with

13

Rama. I read Clarke, and Schmitz, and Anderson, and Chandler, and Dickson and Niven, and Ballard, and Brunner, and Ellison, and Malzberg, and Silverberg, and Spinrad, and so one. Quite a mix, I just liked SF. In the decades since, I have encountered the new authors (especially, back in the day when I subscribed to one or more of the print magazines) that I have added into my constellation and I am still pretty eclectic in my tastes, with a slight lean toward hard SF. I read very little fantasy and I am less forgiving with fantasy than I am with science fiction. I expect a fleshed out world in fantasy and strong character-driven plots (after all, although you are creating a whole new world, it is not a world that has a brand new technology, just classical to early modern technology that may be mixed and matched) -- there should be a sense of history and solid characters. I tend to read good fantasy and only after the work has been established as worthy by the community of readers.

I like Jo Walton's work, in particular the Small Change trilogy, but I have yet to go out and buy Among Others. Primary reason, it is a fantasy novel -- though one could also (I am basing this statement on the backcover blurb) say it is slipstream, which may get me to purchase it post-Christmas.

I wouldn't say that hard SF is less hard today; that depends upon who you are reading. Vernor Vinge and Kim Stanley Robinson are about equal in hardness, but Greg Egan outhards them both. Hard SF does tend to be slightly more character-driven today than in the 1970s and 1980s -- contrast the works of Robert Forward or Geoffrey Landis with those of Peter F. Hamilton and Alastair Reynolds. The more current hard SF also tends to have a better understanding of the social sciences than in the past, which adds to its realism. And yes, everything is darker today. That's just the way things are; we are no longer positive about the future, which tends to grow more grim every day (unless you ignore all news except that which has to do with celebrity, shopping, and gadgets). It is not surprising to have this reflected back in our art, especially in the genre that is expected to deal with exploring the future. And it is really hard to even grasp what the near future is going to be like; case in point, as of this year, it is now possible to 3-D print a working firearm -- what does that do to gun control? How do we contain the American insanity to their side of the border now that anyone with a 3-D printer can download the blueprints for an automatic weapon and have one made in their own home? ***

I am not falling out with fandom as we know it, just some of the older fanzine fans who are coming across as grump old pharts who can't seem to deal with the fact that fandom changes as time goes on, and they seem stuck in time, and fandom is moving on without them. I am finding it myself, and attempting not to be left behind, so we are moving forward with new interests, and making new friends. I have used the term passive consumer to describe more modern fans, while the fans you refer to are more active and constructive.

Any literature should be fun. If it is good enough and lucky enough to have an interactive fandom like SF does, all the better, but fun still has to come with it. And, any common interest that a large number of people share will often generate an interactive fandom. SF fans fooled themselves for many years that they were unique. Any group that can trace itself back to the 1930s will do that, I suppose, but there are fandoms for many interests, SF or otherwise.

*** I have had a peek within Fanstuff in recent months and now better understand what Taral has tried to articulate to me -- however, I still cannot accept his argument. He is not going to change his point of view on fandom any more than a "hard-Gard", Long Island Gardnerian Witch would be willing to accept that the Alexandrian Tradition is a valid tradition of the Craft. That it is all well and fine for Taral and his social group of trufen to set up their boundaries of exclusivity; at present, it still remains a free country. It is also their right to claim that they are the only real fans and everybody else is a fakefan. However, they should not expect the majority -- who actually self identify themselves as being fans (regardless of how they have been designated by some trufen clique) and have some investment in that identity -- to agree with the locked in a temporal warp view of a small minority.

I continue to work with defining the boundary between genre consumer and fan. A year ago, I thought it was quite simple; but, it is not. In 2013, I intend to collect data (or attempt to) from this segment of the population. ***

Polaris is its past format the past 15 years or so is dead. I think they were losing money while trying to compete with the

pro-run cons in terms of guests of honour. The relaxicon seems to
be a little nebulous; I think they don't really have a relaxicon
model to follow, so they are playing it by ear. More has been
planned for the Whocon they advertise, and they have set a
weekend in November 2013 for that. I wouldn't really call Ad
Astra a big-tent event, but they have slightly changed their
focus over the years; they catered to the literary audience, and
they still do, to a lesser extent. SFContario is nearly
exclusively literary, and I think they do a better job. Ad Astra
has the advantage of being the first convention in the spring,
and acts as a springboard for the rest of the local cons to
advertise, and for local fans to shake off some cabin fever.

The locol...I think Canadian fandom was always fragmented, or
Balkanized was the word I used, and that was just because of the
geography. We tried to bring the local fandoms together when we
assembled an interested group for the Toronto in 2003 Worldcon
bid, and that held many fans together for a while, but many will
today say that Worldcon is not their big annual convention, and
they have no interest at all, but they will aim their calendars
and wallets at San Diego Comicon, or DragonCon, or Fan eXpo.

*** We will see how things go with TCON. I still see Ad Astra as a mixed
literary-other media fan-run event nowadays, whether you call that big-tent or not
is semantics -- they are attempting to appeal to everybody without going that final
step and bringing in actor guests. SFContario is definitely a literary SF
convention. Canadian fandom has suffered from regionalism in the past due to
geography, demographics, and language. Today, like society itself, everything is
more fragmented (I tend not to like the term Balkanised as it implies that the
fragments are hostile to one another and unco-operative, when they may just be
indifferent to one another and unco-operative). Toronto as a geographic centre
appears throughout fan history to have been Balkanised. But other geographic
centres have been able to have greater unity. As I said in the last issue, many of
the younger fans do not view the face-to-face social networking of a fan-run
convention as being important -- they want the programming that they cannot get
via social media or elsewhere online -- that is why they prefer events like FanExpo.
***

Bring on that new survey, and we'll respond to it. Looks like you
will have a table at SFContario again. Ah, but will you have a

pith helmet? If you need one, I expect there might be a dealer in the dealers' room who could sell you one.

I blethered on again, I see. Added column-inches for you. We might be pretty busy at SFContario, but we will definitely see you there.

Yours, Lloyd Penney

*** Thanks for blethering, otherwise, this time around we would have no LoC column. See you both at SFContario... ***

Endnote: Acceptances...

Neil Jamieson-Williams

Neil Jamieson-Williams Acceptance Speech for Winning the Elron Award for Worst Fanzine

Hey Scummos,

It is with fucking turgid thoughts that I viddy your malenky gullivers burning brain cells all crispy-like to come to the bezoomy decision to give this award to SWILL. It has been starry temporal wait. I would like to thank the SMOEs and re-commit to continue our original mission; to keep tolchocking fandom. Thank you, you vonny twits, and good night.

Neil Jamieson-Williams Acceptance Speech for Winning the Faned Award for Best Fanzine

Greetings,

To the Canadian Fanzine fanac Award Society, I would like to thank you for this honour. I would also like to thank Lester Rainsford for his great wisdom and perceptive analysis, Arne Hannover for being present, Andrew Hoyt for his inane nattering and phoney British accent and being a toadspawn (which is only normal for one who is a chemist), John Goobly for his tales of the colonial office and bad typing, and I would also like to thank the following persons, tossers, and swine, beginning with... what, I'm out of time!!! Fuck off

#16   Winter 2013

Table of Contents

SWILL is published quarterly (Spring, Summer, Autumn, and Winter) along with an annual every February - in other words, five times per year.

SWILL

Issue #16 Winter 2012

Copyright © 1981 - 2012 VileFen Press

a division of Klatha Entertainment an Uldune Media company

swill.uldunemedia.ca

Back cover by Taral

Editorial: Barbarians at the Gate...

It is the day after Yule and three days before Christmas and I am still ticked off, pissed off, and frustrated by the latest round of American insanity. Frustrated, as there is nothing that I, as a Canadian, can do about this madness next door. It is not my business, I will be told. Shut up, you pinko from Soviet Canukistan! And, I should just avert my eyes and pretend that there is nothing unwholesome going on.

Well, fuck that!

I will not debate the American constitution and differences of interpretation as to the Second Amendment; it has been done before and these arguments have no impact on the troglodytic multitude that believe that the American founding fathers desired every citizen to be armed to the teeth. Logic, statistics, facts, none of these have any effect on the crypto-fascist NRA-loving morons who have made America what it is.

So, this will be an editorial running on emotion as this is the only information that these swine may be capable of processing.

So here we go. Americans are idiots. You daft Yanks think that one is only free if one is armed. The more weapons you have, the safer you are, the more free you are. That it is perfectly normal to own assault weapons, automatic weapons, and light anti-tank weapons for home defence. That is completely ordinary to allow private armies to operate within your borders and not only good for freedom, but a tax savings too.

This Yank attitude and perception does not result in freedom, safety, or order; it creates chaos. Chaos is not a friend to liberty or safety, it is their enemy. It creates a Hobbsian war of all against all and is detrimental to civil society and human rights. Of course, that is the American way; individual rights are primary over collective rights. And the only way to insure that you can exercise your individual rights to the fullest is to be as fully armed as possible. It is a stupid form of democracy, an unbalanced form of democracy, a destabilised form of democracy.

Although I have never seen footage of this on television or YouTube, home invasions in the USA must be military operations carried out by criminals (giving a new meaning to organised crime) using armoured personnel carriers and bazookas and automatic weapons if the average citizen requires anti-tank weapons and machine guns to defend their homes.

And though I have seen this in real life (I used to hunt back in the eighties), I have never approved of it; using automatic weapons for hunting. I do not view the act of machine-gunning down a deer to be the 'sport' the NRA claims that it is. But then, I am just some commie Canadian bow-hunter. What would I know about the thrill of being a real man as you waste a buck with your Bushmaster AR-15?

As some sort of pinko, how could I possibly understand that the existence of private armies is a cornerstone of capitalism at its best, a step in reducing government, lowers the tax burden on the average citizen, and increases freedom? In my benighted soviet-style perception I only see private armies as a potential threat to democracy; private armies, aka mercenaries, do what the money tells them to do.

As a non-resident foreign alien, one can only shake their head at American folly.

Unfortunately, America is a mess that we, here in Canada, will eventually probably have to pick up. Superpowers do not last forever; the USA is a superpower now in decline. While it is possible that the USA may transition to middle power status gracefully, like the French and the British. It is more possible that the move to middle power status will be more like that of the fall of the Soviet Union, ungraceful and messy, but not catastrophic. And it is equally probable that the USA will fall apart like the Ottoman Empire and Yugoslavia -- leaving behind a collection of warring independent states all heavily armed and with nuclear weapons. If we are not dragged down with them (a definite probability) we will be left with this mess on our border; as the next biggest kid on the regional block, the duty to sort this will fall on us, and it will be a dangerous and difficult task.

Thrashing Trufen Quotations from Chairman Taral

Neil Jamieson-Williams

I would like to cover a couple of statements made over the past year by Taral regarding SWILL and myself.

Askance 27
Whither Fanzines?
(Lloyd and Taral are discussing crudzines and at one point Taral writes) '...The absolute worst sin against the reader, however, can be laid on the doorstep of one fan editor who has been told many times that his preferred font makes the eyes water, but he insists the font is sophisticated meta-fannishness and will go on using "Pudmonkey" even if it drives us blind. …or we just stop reading his zine. Do you suppose that's actually his goal?'

Broken Toys #10
Three's the Charm
(an con report for SFContario 3 within which Taral discusses the panel that we were both on) 'The panel was on fanzines and fanzine writing, and the other participants were Chris Garcia (the moderator), Neil Jamieson-Williams and myself... But he (Neil) also publishes a fanzine using a type font that literally cannot be read, and consciously rejects any illustration or layout tricks that would make the experience of reading Swill more pleasurable - a "punk" attitude if ever there was one.'

Well, as I said last issue, SWILL is a crudzine. It always was and always will be. This is not going to change. The lack of any illustrations, other than the front cover, is an editorial choice. The flexibility on this issue would be if someone out there were to produce a comic strip (B&W) that fit the spirit of SWILL; I would run it. However, I have no intention of running illustrations just to cover up empty space. Same goes for layout tricks. Those who have seen the old BCSFAzines that I edited will know that I am quite capable of doing a good layout -- and that fitted BCSFAzine -- but, it does not fit SWILL. Thus, no fancy layout. Is this an example of 'meta-fannishness' as stated by Taral in Askance 27 or is it an example of 'a "punk" attitude'? I would argue in favour of the latter. (Though I am slightly confused as to my status in Taral's perception as to fannishness -- with Taral I am sometimes a fan and sometimes not...) Regardless, the attitude is an early 1980s punk attitude; the layout, style of illustration (when present), and content reflect that attitude.

On the subject of the Pudmonkey font (yet again)... While both Lloyd and Taral can be forgiven for their comments in Askance 27 -- the material was based upon correspondence that I am fairly certain occurred prior to the change to the VT Corona font -- the same cannot be said for Taral's comments in Broken Toys #10. In issue #12 (February 2012), it was announced that SWILL would be moving to the VT Corona font for content and that Pudmonkey would remain for article titles and the ToC. Also in that same issue, the final article was in VT Corona. There is no way that the new font can be described as one 'that literally cannot be read'. Therefore, it would appear that Chairman Taral is still complaining about the Pudmonkey font. Now, it is true that I have continued to use the Pudmonkey font in my responses in the LoC section of the zine -- I have done so in 14 point which (for someone who needs reading glasses himself) is quite readable. It is also true that I used Pudmonkey in last issue's Editorial; this was an aesthetic choice as part of the emphasis of the editorial was on SWILL winning the Elron Award for Worst Fanzine for using the Pudmonkey font.

Askance 27
Whither Fanzines?
(Taral and Lloyd are discussing my motivations for pubbing the revived SWILL; Taral writes) '...I could say that you-know-who is now pissing us off professionally… but I met him at SFContario and found him a reasonable and friendly guy. Now if only he could get over the annoying habit of assuming his degree in sociology gives him a superior perspective for observing fandom, he might have something constructive to say about it.'

Broken Toys #10
Three's the Charm
(Taral desribes me for those who have no idea as to who I am -- which would be the majority) 'Neil I described as the "Punk Academic of Fandom," which does need explanation. Neil is a sociologist who feels a duty to describe fandom to itself in a way that would make his fellow academics happy, using words like "matriliteral," "polyfrenetic," and "diverse etherealcentrism,"

which mean little more than we already know about ourselves but sound vastly more educated.'

Now, I have responded to Taral and Lloyd's comments made in Askance 27 that have appeared in Askance 28 (though I also put my foot into it -- more on that in the LoC article). Okay; I hold advanced degrees in both sociology and in anthropology. It is true that I do not have my PhD, and I don't know if I will ever be able to do so until I retire (the academic institution that I am employed by has some rather unacademic attitudes -- I have to apply for and receive permission from senior management to even apply to do research PhD part-time and to date my requests have been denied). Regardless, I made a decision after completing my Masters degrees to start a career in one of the provincially funded community colleges in Ontario as well as to start a family. At that time, my academic institution had not instituted the draconian policies that exist presently, and I thought that I would have no issue doing a research PhD part-time when I was ready to do so. Note: although most of my teaching is done at a different academic institution that the academic institution I am employed by is partnered with, these policies are those of my employer, not the institution that I do most of my work for. Long story short; I have advanced degrees in two related disciplines and I identify myself as an anthropologist who is also a qualitative sociologist.

As for my perspective being 'superior'; it isn't. Is it more academic and professional and clinical; it is. And FYI, if you think that what appears in SWILL is too academic, wait till you read the final product. Now, I have admitted within this zine (more than once) that I have been out of fandom for a long time -- like 23 and one half years. I have also stated that while gafiated I continued to be a reader and viewer of SF. I have also said that from the perspective of some members of Traditional fandom, I never was and am not now a fan and from other members of Traditional fandom I was a fan but am one no longer -- Taral seems to cross back and forth between these two viewpoints regarding myself. Within a regional context, it would appear that the Vancouver Traditional fandom perspective that I am a fan who was one of them, who gafiated, and has recently returned as a minimally active fan or as a marginal fan. Stepping back into a subculture that you were once a strong member of after almost a quarter of a century can be disorienting as to identity; especially when there is a lack of consensus.

Now, part of the reason for reviving SWILL was to have the zine serve partially as a dialogue between the researcher and the researched. So, I don't go off creating ideal types based entirely on my own observations that are not grounded within the subculture being studied. And, at the end of the day, I have to be able to communicate those observations with academe as well as the educated layperson, if my research is to be truly successful. It also has to be inclusive to the entire subculture as it presently exists -- not how it was in 1970, or 1980, etc. So, yes; I have to use academic terminology (not Taral's made up terms) as I attempt to construct categories that will lead to ideal types. The lack of consensus as to who is and is not a fan is one of the problems I have to solve in this research and it is one that (in a way has always existed within the subculture) is even more difficult at present as I have stepped back into fandom during a period of transition brought about by technological change and a definite generation gap. Had I begun this study even ten years ago, this would have been quite different; present, but nowhere near as pronounced as it is today. While this does make for a more interesting research environment, it also presents an increased level of difficulty.

The participation in this dialogue can assist in the final study being one that actually does reflect SF fandom as it is in the second decade of the 21st century. Simply pooh-poohing the entire notion of an academic study of SF fandom or demanding that the study only focus upon your niche within SF fandom is just not productive, period. It doesn't stop the research from happening and only will result in your particular niche not being represented. It is even less productive to insist that the researcher use a particular niche's definition of fandom (more so when there exists no definitional consensus within that niche) for all of fandom; especially when that niche represents only a small segment of the entire SF fan subculture.

As I said above, I have revived SWILL partially for the reason of dialogue with the SF fan subculture. I have also done so because I like pubbing fanzines -- my type of fanzine. If the sole reason for SWILL was just to engage in this dialogue, I wouldn't be writing several thousand words five times a year that were superfluous to that dialogue.

Pissing on a Pile of Old Amazings:

...a modest column by Lester Rainsford

Here's a con report. Swilol does not do con reports. Swill is
irreverent and doesn't follow rules. Therefore here's a con
report. It's a Swill thing to do~~t and~~ this kind of intellectual
bravery that garnered Swill a brace of awards, folks!

Right, we're talking SFContario 2012. Far as Lester knows it's
the third of its kind, but the old Underwood doesn't have a
googles so that's that.

Years and years ago, Lester was permanently ~~traumatized scarred~~
amused and outraged at nearly being run down by a couple of
phaser-wielding fans in start rek red univorms charging around
the halls of Maplecon. Which was Ottawa around 1981 if memory
serves. The fact that this incident is vividly rememberd still is
a fine indication of how ~~traumatic~~amusing it was. The fact that
the fans barely fit into their red uniforms added the extra spice
of real danger, as in cows are pretty placid and usually fear
humans, but if one charges you you7'd better get out of the way
darm quick.

Well, Lester has to apologise to those fans at Mapelcon. They
brough energy to the con. SFContario would surely have been a bit
livelier had there been some star trek geeks charging rhough the
halls ~~wavig~~ wavingphasers.

Now, there was no issue with the panels, which Lester likes to
attend. Even if there were a few of the local blowhards on
certain panels whose ideas lester has heard before, in quite loud
detail, before. Same ideas. You get the point. Mostly, the panels
were lively, and there was an odd, but good, dosconnect in that
panel memobers were ~~quite of m~~ostly young. HOwever, the hallways
of the con tended to be either empty, or contain one or two
wheezing, old, fat, folk. I.e. fans.

(so, if you are a young fan, and have weight issues, take care of them, or you will be an old fan with weight issues, and that doesn't look like any sort of fun to Lester.)

The trouble is, if you can barely make it up a few stairs and across a bridge to the next panel or event, how much energy do you have to actually , you know, do stuff at the con? The answer,is, not so much. Lwster would have oliked to stay around atfter 9pm, but there seemeed to be zero reason to do so unless the hotels sad-sack bar appealed. And if it did appeal, there were other places much more lively in the enighbourhood. So it was home, on the GO train or by car, which is kind of disappointing.

"No no no you wieghtist chauvinist, those people may be full-bodies, but they're still sharp as tacks!" the peanut gallery repsonds. Well, maybe, yes, they still are very good at what they do. However, the energy to think new thoughts and modify your point of view gets harder and harder as the energy flags. The inhabitants of an old-age home might be abhave sharp meomory and be shrewed, but changing their mind isn ot going to happen. You will hear the same stories, and maybe even word-=for-word, every time. So all respect to the fans and professionals in SF who still do their thing, but geez, has their 'thing' changed much since 1979?

It would be an interesting survey to see if the fans who come to conventions are the healthiest fans out there, with the lests healthy just staying in their basements. On the other hand, perhaps sf attracts the halt and lame, so that the poopulation of sf fans and readers is less healthy and more obese than the general population. If only The Swill was a sociologist instead of an anthropologist, we may get answers to these question. Because that's what sociologists do. And not anthropologists, to Lester's best knowledge.

While it is unclear what the costume fans and the media fans really bring to the inteleccua intellectual content of a con, there is no doubt that they do bring some life, even if the steampunk googles and top hats are getting kind of old. (Heaven preserve us if twilight or Justin Beaver becomes the next costume trend.) Heck even some fans moving at a pace faster than a sleepy turtle would have made the con space feel a little less like the old age home after a big thursday meal, i.e. no bingo tonight so it's straight to bed and don't make any noise you whippernsapper punks.

And now, if you are thoroughly pissed ~~ant~~ at this pissing column, come to the ~~kaffeksasch~~ ~~kaffeklasetch~~ Swill panel and let us know.

We brough, and left, a big bag of day-old donuts on the table for YOU, our enthusiastic followers. Where were you?? (Okay we'll bring 'Posutm' next time too.)

(Okay, piling the old Analogs and S&SF's upside down didn't fool anyone either. Despite the cheesy '70s ads on the back, revelaed to all to see, they were no Amazings. Lester apologises fully and completely. It's getting harder and harder to get a pile of old Amazings to piss on. 'Death of fandom! Details at eleven.")

Flogging a Dead Trekkie:

The American Weigh; or, a Gram of Brains is Worth a Pound of Shit

(1981 reprint)

P. I. Leninski

A lot of Americans believe a lot of silly things; but, as Abraham Lincoln pointed out, you can fool some of the people all of the time. And, as H. L. Menken once said, no-one went bankrupt underestimating the intelligence of the American public.

So it should not be too surprising to see that Libertarianism is quite popular down in the States. This typically American (read: brainless) philosophy is puffed up to ridiculous proportions in L. N. Smith's book The Probability Broach.

There are no doubt people who haven't read this book. There are also people who have never fallen into a sewer; both classes can consider themselves lucky.

Is this book sf? No. It is propaganda. Beside this book, Mein Kampf seems reasonable, lucid, and logical. The writing style is dismal, the characters cardboard, and the plot preposterous.

For those of you not swimming about in sewers, let me outline what this book is about.

In 1987, the U.S. is in sad shape. It is in dismal shape. We are then shown a Libertarian world where everything is WONDERFUL.

Moral. Libertarianism is WONDERFUL.

Ha ha. Hee hee. Ho ho.

For instance, in the Libertarian world (henceforth to be called OZ) science is WONDERFUL. The only trouble is that Ms. Smith knows as much about science as a Californian knows about igloos. The science in this story is not Omni-level; it is Scientology level (Sorry, Mr. Hubbard). (Well, not _really_ sorry). Why science in a Libertarian world would progress faster is difficult to see. Note that Einstein came up with relativity, the photo-electric effect, and E=Mc2 while working in a patent office. A _Swiss Government_ patent office.

Would Maxwell have thought of the electromagnetic equations earlier if he wasn't being taxed?

In fact, the science in this story is all gadgetry. For instance, 'electrically heated streets' are mentioned. A simple, back-of-the-envelope calculation shows that to melt the snow off the streets in a medium-sized city would require a steady power drain on the order of a gigawatt.

Perhaps they have never heard of snow shovels. Of course, these _are_ Libertarians.

Other curiosities abound, such as fusion powered dirigibles travelling at 500km/hr. Perhaps Ms. Smith has never considered the etymology of 'dirigible'. It means 'not rigid'. A kilometre-long dirigible travelling at half a megametre and hour would quickly become like a patchwork quilt: one patch here, another one there, and several more patches elsewhere.

This should not be surprising. Americans are conscious, subconsciously, of their abysmal lack of culture and sophistication, and so they tend to retreat into gadgetry. ('We're not barbarians - we invented whitewall tires!!!) Sure. And Attila's men decorated their horses, you know.

That's the trouble with this book: it makes no convincing case that OZ will be WONDERFUL.

It simply says so. I'm sorry, but this is nonsense. I could write a book where penguins have taken over the world. I, too, could claim that it was going to be WONDERFUL.

Oh, well, The Probability Broach was written for believers anyway. For nonbelievers, have you ever considered a penguin for a boss? Unless we accept it on blind faith, we clearly see that OZ would not work.

There is another neat thing: the perverted emphasis on guns. It seems that guns solve every problem. Just think how wonderful it is to have your own gun. Is someone blocking the elevator door? Bang! Is someone sitting in the washroom too long? THROW A NUCLEAR HAND GRENADE OVER THE PARTITION!! BOOOM!!!

Or art criticism: "Dali sucks." Bang! Pow!

Yes, Americans love guns. It is, of course, their constitutional right to bear arms. A pity, though, that they have no right to carry brains; and most of them don't.

People like President Reagan are against gun control. This is why others shoot them. With guns.

Americans, in fact, seem to think that firepower solves everything. Just look at El Salvador. These idiot Yanks think that, by propping up a murderous, repressive, anti-freedom, right-wing junta (pronounced 'yunta'), they are making the world 'safe for democracy'. Safe for American multi-nationals, in any case.

Isn't American democracy wonderful? Don't we all wish to preserve the American Way of Life: Jack Ruby, Charles Manson, Richard Nixon, Son of Sam, 1,096 murders in Detroit, lynchings, murders, intolerance, Monkey Trials, motherhood, and apple paie.

Look, you stuoid Americans. Why don't you take your offensive, moronic gospel shows, which actually clutter up Canadian airwaves, and stick them where a Chihuahua can't see? Why don't you take your buses with the golden eagle on the front, and turn them into roosts for pigeons? And old-time preachers? Takey your flag, your Pledge of Allegiance (no, not Lemon Pledge), and your whole damn 'grey-hat nay-ha-shun', and rotate it through n-space, so your asses wind up where your ears are (but who will notice?).

Observe that even Kalahari bushmen have progressed beyond the stage America is at today.

Smarten up, America, or you'll be sorry: do you see any Neanderthals about today???

Scribbling on the Bog Wall:
Letters of Comment

Neil Jamieson-Williams

As I write this, there is only a single LoC and a semi-LoC this time around. My comments are, of course, in glorious pudmonkey.

1706-24 Eva Rd.
Etobicoke, ON
M9C 2B2

December 8, 2012

Dear Neil:

Thanks for Swill 15. This might be pretty quick, the daytime job is keeping me busy, and weekend spare time is rare, but here goes with a loc, see what we can agree upon.

Two fan awards? Excellent! Worst Fanzine and Best Fanzine? I'd say you're doing everything you might want to do with Swill...offend lots of people, and inform lots of people, and that means you've got lots of readers. You must still be scratching your head over this, but take the egoboo, and run.

Thanks, Lloyd. SWILL obviously offends some and informs others -- though I doubt that I have a lot of readers. Perhaps, I do, and only a select few send in LoCs. Anyway, it is hyper-cool to win awards for the best and the worst in the same year...

I have been a fan of SF fandom, but as time goes on...well, not so much. When I write my letters, I send them off to the fan editor, and then I archive them on a LiveJournal account. A few people access that account from time to time, and they make some comments on what I have to say, and there's a new level of communications, to me, anyway. A couple of years ago, one self-appointed judge (with no real authority) said that what I was doing was publishing before the faned I sent the letter to could do so, and it was horrible and unfannish, and how could I do such a bad thing, and I would never again receive any fanzines from him. (The fact he hadn't produced any fanzines in years was not lost on me.) I related this story recently, and two more self-appointed judges attacked me, saying I was publishing before the faned could do so, how could I do something so unfannish, etc. I thought that I was archiving and not publishing, for it was not yet part of a formal publication, and I was attacked for that, and then I said that we would have agree to disagree, and I was attacked further. Most faneds know I do this, and don't mind. All rights revert to the author, after all. But nothing would have happened, and no one would have noticed, if I just hadn't said anything about my LJ archive at all. Fandom is relatively anarchical, but those self-appointed judges will rise to try to impose their own order on things, to impose what they think is the way Things Should Be Done. I left a couple of Facebook groups, and I am carrying on as usual. Over my 35 years of fandom, I sometimes move from one interest to another, and sometimes, they overlap... conrunning, costuming, fanzines, others. Fanzines are still fun, but those judges make it less so. They wonder why there aren't more people involved in fanzines, and they only need to look in a mirror to see what the biggest problem is.

Okay, I had noticed that several months ago when I Googled SWILL and scrolled through the links. Personally, I don't see archiving your LoCs on LiveJournal as being a problem, period. As we both know, that would be a different situation if you were being paid for this writing. However, you are not; therefore there is no issue, in my opinion. As for being unfannish; I am afraid that I am probably the last person to go to for determining what is and what is not fannish. I can discuss this using courtesy as the basis; if there is an issue that was being strongly debated in issue 86 of fanzine X and you write a letter of comment on this issue for issue 87, it is probably good form not to publish it elsewhere until issue 87 comes out. As for defining publish, I don't see archiving the LoC on LiveJournal as publishing -- with a general search this LoC that I am responding to shows up around page 17, in other words, you have to make a specific search e.g. SWILL Lloyd Penney for it to come upon the first search page. I really don't see the conflict here.

As for self-appointed judges, they exist in every subculture I have studied and/or been a member of. The anarchic nature of fandom allows for these self-appointed judges to exert power in the form of being the determiners of who is a fan and the Way Things Should Be Done. They are a pain in the ass. As I have mentioned previously, this sort of behaviour is why I fully gafiated in 1986; I didn't have time for this sort of shit and it didn't make being involved in the SF fan community worth it. It think that the Traditional fans are the most guilty of this behaviour, the desire to roll the clock back to 1980 or 1970, that anyone who is not of their cohort is not a fan; this has a detrimental impact on younger people getting involved in fanzines.

There are fans everywhere. Science fiction, in the form of the industry it has become, has become multi-faceted, and anyone can enjoy the smallest facet. Yet, in our own insecurity, we push others away, say those we see beneath us aren't fannish enough, and we insult and ignore them. Very fannish, unfortunately, and not just in SF fandom, but just about any
interest out there that allows a subculture of its fans to gather. This is more of a psychological problem humanity has, and not just fans.

I am a traditional and active fan, I haven't always been involved in fanzines, I enjoy costuming and I've retired from conrunning. In the long run, you've got to find the fun you want. I think it's a good idea to know the history of fandom, to see where it arose from, but we've got to have the chance to make our own history. Generally, I try to be constructive. There are too many around me who try to be destructive, and they are one of the reasons why traditional fandom's numbers are indeed dwindling. In the long run, who'd want to hang out with that sour bunch?

Essentially ditto. It is also how I see things. Though I also will tweak the nose and give a kick to the yarbles to that same sour bunch.

The "big-tent" idea of conventions serving fannish interests may have been the most successful of all the convention formats. As these monster shows were starting to gain in size, fannish conventions were splitting interests off themselves as those interests demanded more time, space and money at conventions, and when those conventions either wouldn't or couldn't cater to those interests, new specialty conventions would form, catering mostly or exclusively to that interest. Fannish cons split to cater to single interests, and monster cons built up to serve a majority of the fandom.

I agree. Though, here in southern Ontario, it would seem that the competition between the commercial trade show conventions is beginning to cause damage to the big-tent fan-run conventions.

The locol…I am sure I am a fakefan to some. Your mileage may vary, as they say. We all take out of science fiction fandom and all related activities what we enjoy, and leave the rest for others.

I found out Polaris' problem was not with money, but with labour. They simply could not run a convention that size with dwindling numbers of people will to serve on the committee, or to serve as gophers and other staff. We've retired from running cons, others have given up, some got married to each other, others step away from the increasing attentions of life and trying to make a living.

That's interesting. It differs from what was said in the TCON email just prior to the con and what gophers/staff were saying at the convention. However, it is a reason that also makes sense; loss of volunteer staff can kill an organisation.

Gone on for almost two pages, I have…not bad. It's been a very busy day, and this is the first bit of relaxation I've had. Take care, have yourself a great Christmas, and see you next year.

Yours, Lloyd Penney.

Happy Holidays to you both and all the best for 2013…

(John is commenting on my LoC on Askance 27. As John is in the final stages of his PhD and has placed Askance on hiatus until the summer, I am going to comment back here in SWILL now.)

Wow! Now this is a meaty loc with a lot of matter to chew on and digest... Also, since you mention that you have degrees in anthropology and sociology, those provide you with a background into understanding cultural creation and assimilation, but I would not have said they give you "a superior perspective to observe fandom through." That word "superior" carries a ton of connotative meaning, such as you consider yourself to be "superior" or "better than" most fans. That kind of an attitude is going to piss people off, definitely. However, judging from the context in which you said that, I suspect you mean that your degrees in those subjects gives you technical information that provides you with a more professional and objective appraisal of the fannish subculture. Since many fans carry graduate degrees and don't wave them about like banners at the head of a phalanx of foot soldiers, consider this a lengthy word of warning on my part...

Hi John,

I agree. I was sloppy, there. I was reacting to Taral and used his choice of words, i.e. "superior". I will back off on mentioning my degrees after this issue of SWILL. There now appears to be little probability of ever convincing Taral that academic research on fandom is something that should allowed to happen. Too bad, he would make a good source.

Good luck on the last push... Will also write a LoC for Askance 29.

Neil

Endnotes And the Winner is...

Neil Jamieson-Williams

So here are the final results of the poll for which Canadian SF convention shall be razrezed on the back cover of SWILL 17.

- **Ad Astra 2012**   53
- CanCon 2012   1
- Con*Cept 2012   0
- Hal-Con 2012   1
- Keycon 29   0
- Polaris 26   27
- Sci-Fi on the Rock 6   0
- SFContario 3   6
- VCON 37   14
- When Words Collide 2012   2

And so, stay tuned for SWILL 17, the 2012 Annual and what we do to Ad Astra...

Canadian Fanzine Fanac Awards

The Faned

Presented at VCon 37, Sept. 2012

Best Fanzine of 2011

Rudmonkey Guy

#17   Annual 2013

Table of Contents

SWILL is published quarterly (Spring, Summer, Autumn, and Winter)
along with an annual every February - in other words, five times
per year.

SWILL

Issue #17 Annual 2013

Copyright © 1981 - 2013 VileFen Press

a division of Klatha Entertainment an Uldune Media company

swill.uldunemedia.ca

Editorial: I'm Tardy; So?!

James William Neilson

By the time this issue is uploaded, the SWILL Annual will be two months late. While, I am usually very good at meeting deadlines, I am not always good at meeting my own deadlines (i.e. one's that I have imposed upon myself which I will only disappoint myself if I fail to achieve them). SWILL is very tardy; and your problem is? It's not like you paid a subscription and the zine didn't arrive on time as expected; it's free and you are not a customer (certainly not a paying customer).

In some circles, zine tardiness carries with it an aura of fannishness. In other circles -- e.g. the Fanstuff Set -- it only serves as evidence of my lack of commitment to fandom and hence my inherent unfannishness. I guess it all depends upon the eye of the perceiver. As the first week of April dawned and SWILL being over a month late I did have some minor anxiety of this state of affairs. However, that miniscule uneasiness quickly evaporated on the road to Ad Astra.

During the hurley burley of getting out the door to an early morning meeting at work before heading to far Markham, I forgot my Kobo at home. Though, I did have my Kindle. However, I am not a major Kindle user, for a variety of reasons that have more to do with Amazon than the technology. I was an early adopter of the Kobo and still use my first generation Kobo which as over 350 books on it. My Kindle was packed to go since it is later generation technology that allows me to surf the net if free WiFi is available on a much bigger screen (albeit monochrome) than my smart phone. Why this is important is that while there are numerous magazines on my Kindle, there is only one book. That book being Breakfast in the Ruins: Science Fiction in the Last Millennium by Barry Malzberg. For those SWILL readers who have failed to notice that Malzberg's essays in Science Fiction Review (many of which made their way into The Engines of the Night: Science Fiction in the Eighties -- reprinted as the first half of Breakfast in the Ruins) had a major influence on me and the SWILL attitude, let me come clean; they did.

So with the QEW backlogged for no other reason than Oakville volume the one hour trip from downtown Hamilton to downtown Toronto became a two hour trek. Plus, I still had another hour and thirty minutes to travel by TTC to the back of beyond, aka

Markham. Thus, I had a long stroll down memory lane as I re-read
The Engines of the Night and any issues/concerns of fannish
identity or even the importance of fannish identity dissipated in
the harsh light of Engines.

It didn't fucking matter.

I have attempted to excavate from my wetware what the fannish
perception was of The Engines of the Night when it first came out
back in 1982, but memory fails me. I do recall that the book was
controversial, that many of the pros didn't like it, so it would
be fair to speculate that many fans also didn't like Engines.
After all, it was very critical of science fiction and contained
criticism of science fiction editors and writers, as well as some
pull-no-punches shots at science fiction fandom. But what the
general fan view of this book was back in the day, I cannot
recall; it wasn't important enough to be saved to my permanent
mental archives or, if it was, has long since been overwritten by
more important data. The only recollection I can extract is a
vague memory of some Big Name Fan (not that big name as I cannot
recall their name or physical features, just a still visible tag
that they were supposed to be someone of importance but not a
writer or editor) made a comment about my copy of Engines (and I
actually bought the hardcover) saying, "Why are you reading that
shit?" Thing is, I didn't think that it was shit and I actually
think that a lot of it was fucking brilliant, and some of it was
not very interesting. Malzberg has his hobby horses and axes
being ground and some of them are of interest, to me, and some of
them are not. It is very obvious that the Fifties were important
to the genre and to Malzberg. They really aren't very important
to me and my perception of the genre other than the historical
impact of the implosion of the pulp magazine market at the close
of that decade. So, overall, I liked Engines then, and I still
like it today and I like Engines better than the second half of
Breakfast in the Ruins, though that probably has more to do with
nostalgia than actual critical review.

So reading Engines en route to attend a science fiction
convention, may add distortion to the reader's bias or may bring
the reader's focus into sharp clarity. Bottom line, crux-of-the-
matter, is that really, when you really and honestly think about
it, science fiction doesn't matter. Science fiction is never
going to "save the world". Science fiction is very rarely ever
predictive. While it has the potential to inspire technological
development, and the potential to offer cautionary tales, and the
potential to assist the individual to adapt to ever changing
technology, most of the time, it does none of the above. It is

3

just entertainment and escapist entertainment[1] at that. Science fiction is my preferred genre to read, and to watch, and to write and that is not going to change, period. But, although science fiction does have the potential to examine the human experience within the simultaneously expanding and shrinking technosphere that we live within and are completely dependant upon -- with the stage of all time and all places available for its settings -- most of the time, that potential is relinquished, only the veneer is scratched, or worse, forgotten, and what is produced is just another commodity. It isn't important.

And if science fiction isn't important, what does that say about science fiction fandom and the importantness of fannishness?

It says that it is fucking unimportant.

---

[1] Just a note on escapist entertainment. Science fiction is often wrongly tarred with this brush as the only offender. It is not; in particular with our television and film entertainments. Anybody who has seen a real CSI lab, a real emergency ward, a real police station, a real court room will know that what appears on television, and on film, are partial escapes from reality and sometimes strong stretches of reality. Science fiction is singled out because it starts with a purely fictitious reality which places the onus upon it to make that reality appear real -- in television and film this fails more often than not (and we are often more forgiving of a film seen in a cinema on first viewing than we are of a television series that is broken up with commercials).

Thrashing Trufen: Wallowing in the Shallow End...

James William Neilson

Upon arrival at Ad Astra, I got myself checked in, dumped my bag, went down to get my registration package, and set out looking for food. The hotel restaurant made it quite clear that they wanted me to opt for the expensive buffet not a la carte and hotel buffets may be okay for breakfast/brunch but I have yet to have had a good one for dinner. I went off site for some real food and when I returned to the hotel, it being still early -- around 7:30 PM -- I popped into the hotel bar for a drink. There I ran into one of my old droogs and his spouse. They had managed to convince the hotel restaurant to serve them a la carte -- not that I couldn't have, I just decided that my desire to eat expensive crap was low and the effort required to force the issue would be more inconvenient than the effort of walking over to the nearby British pub for some moderately priced, moderately good food. Regardless, I joined them and we immediately and briefly began talking about the convention and fandom before moving onto more important topics such as work, how our kids were doing, outsourcing manufacturing, and 3-D printing. In the short discourse about fandom my droog said this about the average attendee of the convention, "We don't exactly fit this demographic." And I agree.

Even back in secondary school, science fiction fandom (such as I knew it) was not my only social network. I will agree that it was a major part of my social network, but my core social network was my friends and acquaintances who attended the same secondary school. And I also had friends and acquaintances from my part-time job. As a young adult, science fiction fandom was a part of my social network but never my only social network. There was only one time in my life when science fiction fandom was my sole social network, and that was during my first year in Vancouver. I had moved to Vancouver, knowing nobody there, at all -- no friends, acquaintances, or relatives -- and had timed my arrival for the V-Con convention. So although science fiction fandom was my only social network for most of my first year in that city, by the end of the year it had reduced to being my major social

network along with the additional social networks that I had
established.

So, only for a brief moment in time was science fiction fandom
ever my only social network. I don't think that science fiction
fandom has ever been the sole social network for any of my old
droogs.

As for my droog and I, both of us were attending Ad Astra for
less than fannish reasons. True, for both of us, there was the
social aspect of meeting people that one only sees at this type
of event. More so for me, as I live outside of the GTA. Less so
for my droog who does live within the GTA and travels into
Toronto more frequently than I do. Both of us were moderating or
on some panels. However, both of us were attending the
convention for business purposes; for my droog commercial, for me
a mix of academic and commercial. But, at the end of the day,
the convention had a primarily pragmatic purpose with the social
aspect being secondary or tertiary. We were there to promote,
network, sell, and for myself, collect research data.

We certainly were not attending because science fiction fandom is
our primary, or sole, social network. Nor were we attending
because Ad Astra is a major annual event in our social calendars.
It makes you wonder about the people for whom those two last
statements are the affirmative. It calls to mind the quote from
The Engines of the Night, unattributed by Malzberg except by the
tag 'ex-science fictioner' (he is talking about a writer not a
fan), who said, "You know, you can get a great deal of attention,
real reverence at these conventions for sure. But you know when
the trouble begins? It starts when you ask who in hell you're
getting this attention from."

Yeah, I really don't fit this demographic.

Pissing on a Pile of Old Amazings:

...a modest column by Lester Rainsford

Robert "Bob" heinlein had at least two ~~books~~ early books published after his death, For Us the Living a novel, and Tramp Royale a travelogue. Lester is here to summarily dismiss the first, and to make unhappy report of the second.

For us the Living is indigestible, a utopia of the kind you've read before, only by Bob, so there's some kind of swinging involved. Sixty pages of this was all Lester could stomach.

Tramp Royale is a travelogue, and Lester doesn't mind travelogues. However reading this one shows why it was not published in Bob's lifetime. Travelogues can be about the place, or about the writer interacting with the place, but it's got to be interesting. Here's how Tramp Royale goes:

Bob: Rio has the most amazing harbour. San Francisco is nice and Sydney is nice, but Rio is way better. It's fabulous. I won't describe it any further; you must go see it for yourself.

Reader: Well fuck you too Bob.

In fact, other than an interesting visit to the inaccessible island of Tristan da Cunha, well almost visit, there's not much in the way of foreign lands of interest described in the book. However, we do learn a lot about Bobk, and it's not very nice.

Bob's a whiner. Everywhere the cusomst officials have strange customs that would not be tolerated in 1950s Colorado (which calls into question why travel at all?). The British Commonwealth is apparently actively working against the interests and desireds of a fine red-blooded American traveller. Australia sucks. Bob spends pages and pages describing his indescribably awful hotel room in Sydney (this after not telling us nothing about Rio harbour, mind you).

It's not even clear how reliable Bob is. In the Brasilian seciont, he talks about aking a bus that goes through some mountains. The road is modern, it seems, and so is the bus. Bob breezily describes ~~is~~ it as "doing ~~nintely~~ ninety into the mountains, until the road got steeper and it slowed down to seventy". Well, since he also talks about "Ticky" (his annoying name for Virginia) doing nintety at home, he's not exactly talking km per h. Now, in Colorado, maybe if the Heinleins owned a newer Oldsmobile with the Rocket V8, or onte of the hotter Hudson Super Hornets, TIcky may have been able to drive ninety, for a while at least (Lester does not know much about the condition of roads in Colorado in the early 1950s). But sure as shootin', ain't no way a Brasilian bus did 90MPH ~~into the~~ on a flat road, never mind into the mountans. Bob's shittin' us here. Maybe hes shittin' himself at the same time, but for sure he's shittin' us. For someone supposedly with a technical background, this is the kind of exaggerated incorrectness that really calls into wquestion everything else.

The other thing Bob does that doesn't help the travelogue is to potnificate. The politics of Panama, of Chile and Argentina, of South Africa, of Australia and New Zeland ("those commonwealth bastards hate Americans, of course") he explains to us, kind of like Lazarus Long. It gets tiring, and nLester completed the book by not rolling eyes too much at all the explanations Bob provides of How The World Workds. (The world where buses go 90MPH.)

You can also tell that he was a perfect nuisance on a cargo ship (where there's not a whole lot of places to go) to other passengers. He "Shakes the British couple out of their reserve" in a day or two. They must have thought, "there's that horrible American, let's try to be polite and smile". Maybe he suggested wife swapping. It's obviously something he was thinking about back in the 1930s when he wrote <u>For Us the Living</u>.

ALso annoying is the supposition of American superiority because HE FOUND OUT THE NAME OF THE HELP AND ALWAYS USED IT. Unlike the COmmonweathers and other goofballs such as those euro Dutch. After all, if you call the help by their name, it SHOWS that you are superior civilization.

In a few places, Bob devends the McCarthy thing. Feeling devensive any, Bob? The funny thing is that he claims that the people hauled infront of the unamerican activities committee aren't hurt all that much if at all, and after all this is a small price to pay for their 'treason'. He uses that word. How many people actually were convicted of treason before being hauled in front of McCarthy? Lester doesn't think there were a whole lot. Maybe ont even one. Lester also feels that glibly assessing 'treason' is a pretty serious charge, especially in America. The Bob of <u>Starship Troopers</u> is peeking out!

At the very end, instead of summarizing whty he and "Ticky" travelled around the world, and what their experience was, and what they'd seen that was the baset--you know, the things that the reader of a travelogue is interested in--he comes in out of left field (right field?) and declares that America needs to stop apologizing and work for its own interesteds. Be strong, and don't listen to anyone else. Apparently that's the lesson he learned dealing with customs agents in Indonesia or something. The reader things, "well, that will get you through customs qucker if everyone hates you".

Under the veneer of sophistication and worldly wisdon, Bob turns out to be the Ugly American on tour. It's something that the reader of the travelogue grasps, maybe ont immediately, and not for ten or twenty or thirty pages, but the book is almost three hundred pages long and that's plenty enough.

Needless to say Bob has no idea. He's just ~~chai~~ shaking the reticent Brits out of their aloofness. He's just pointing out how much better a hotel room would be in Boulder Colorado or SOmeplace ~~Iowa~~ Idaho than in Australia. Now maybe that's true or not. But as a travel book it's not. Good. As a character study, as penned by an unreliable narrator, <u>of</u> that unreliable narrator, it's probably worth readying.

Maybe Bob was working that angle all along.

~~Mind you, anyone who has read any of his disastrous later books will kind of doubt that.~~

Ha ha! April fools!

(*This column is early.*)

** And this zine is late ed. ;) **

Flogging a Dead Trekkie:

Violating the ~~Taboos~~ Norms of Science Fiction

Part 1 of 8 -- Introduction

James William Neilson

In keeping with The Engines of the Night theme; in the essay "Tell Me Doctor If You Can That It's Not All Happening Again" Malzberg discusses, among other things (like the Fifties), the 7 Taboos of Science Fiction. Well, Malzberg is a bit inconsistent as to whether these are actual "taboos" or "limitations" or "dangerous plots", though he uses the term taboo the most. Regardless, he is talking about story concepts and/or plots that if written -- if the norms are violated -- are unpublishable. No professional editor in the genre will touch these stories with a three-metre pole, and certainly would never, ever publish them.

Here they are, in brief.

NORM VIOLATION ONE: "Bleak, dystopian, depressing material which implies that the present cultural fix is insane or transient and will self-destruct . . . that the very ethos and materials of the society...will bring it down."

NORM VIOLATION TWO: "Material which is highly internalized. That is, science fiction written from the point of view of a meditative and introspective central character whose perceptions are the central facet of the work, whose reactions to the events of the story are more important than the story itself."

NORM VIOLATION THREE: "Science fiction which implies that contemporary accepted mores of sexuality, socioeconomics, or familial patterning might be corrupting, dangerous, or destructive."

NORM VIOLATION FOUR: "Science fiction which owes less to classical, Aristotelian notions of "plot"-the logical, progressive ordering of events as a protagonist attempts to solve a serious and personally significant problem-than "mood"...that is, the events for their own sake..."

NORM VIOLATION FIVE: "Science fiction truly at the hard edge of contemporary scientific investigation..."

NORM VIOLATION SIX: "Science fiction which questions science fiction; work which questions the assumptions of the category and speculates on the effect it might have upon its readership."

NORM VIOLATION SEVEN: "Genuinely feminist science fiction; that is, science fiction in which women are perceived to react to events and internalize in a way which is neither a culturally received stereotype nor a merely male stereotype projected onto female characters."

So, for the next seven issues we are going to play with these themes here in SWILL. Or at least I am going to play with them; we shall have to see if anybody else has an interest. And I am also going to experiment with each of these norm violations or taboos by writing a story that breaks the taboo and see if I can get it published. That will be the challenge.

That means that I am going to go all out and write, what I consider to be, good stories for this experiment. Big deal, you are just some old fan/old fakefan nobody's ever heard of; what makes you think that you can write?

The fact is that, there was a time when people did actually pay me, professional/near professional rates, to write fiction. Not in prose, but for radio and occasionally film. Writing in radio during the Eighties was akin to what Malzberg describes about writing for the pulps back in the Fifties and earlier; you ground the stuff out, often under several pseudonyms, with little time for editing script, numerous re-writes once it got to production, and far more anonymity than that a pulp writer -- at least someone may have old yellowed magazines in their collection that contain one of your stories -- once your radio play is broadcast, unless it is rebroadcast, it's gone.

As for film, many of the film scripts that I wrote never made it beyond Development -- I got paid, but the film was never made. Of the three films that I wrote the original script for that did get made, I received no credit for those scripts; they had been re-written upteen times therefore the original writer's credit drops off as the re-writes go on. Not that I have really cared up until recently, because two of those films sucked so bad in the final product that it didn't really matter and the third was okay but really only the central premise remained of the original script. And yes, I used to be a member of ACTRA, when the writers were part of this union and long before they separated to form the Writers Guild of Canada.

So, can I write prose fiction? Well, let us experiment, shall we...

Scribbling on the Bog Wall:
Letters of Comment

James William Neilson

As I write this, there is only a single LoC this time around. My comments are, of course, in glorious pudmonkey.

From the SMOTE (Secret Master of the Elrons) R. Graeme Cameron - Jan 8th, 2013

Hi Neil!

In SWILL #15 you wrote:

I kind of expected that SWILL would win some sort of Elron this year, and it did. SWILL won "Worst Fanzine" for the use of the pudmonkey font.

What I didn't expect was to receive a Faned -- the Canadian Fanzine Fanac Award -- for "Best Fanzine". This is actually a bit of an honour as it means that at least some people out there like what I am doing, here. It makes a nice counterpoint to those out there who have commented that SWILL is not and never has been a fanzine and that I am not and never have been a fan.

An Elron is awarded tongue-in-cheek as a spoof award and is not meant to be taken seriously. The pudmonkey font seemed to generate the most criticism and, everyone in fanzine fandom being aware of the infamous pudmonkey debate, was the most convenient excuse to award an Elron.

On the other hand the 'Faned' (Canadian Fanzine Fanac Society Award or CFFS Award) is given out on the basis of genuine achievement. SWILL is not only a 'new' zine on the scene (all new zines welcome!) but a breath of fresh air that has shaken up the somewhat stale self-image of Canadian zinedom by injecting new life into the question of what zinedom is all about, indeed, what fandom is all about. Huzzah!

Hi Graeme, as I have stated before, I am rather uncertain as to how widespread in fanzine fandom is the view that SWILL is "a breath of fresh air". I will agree that t but I will agree that the zine does raise "the question of what zinedom is all about".

OF COURSE SWILL counts as a fanzine (though it may have other definitions, research tool for instance) and of course you were and are a fan. You edited BCSFAzine from issue #108 (May 1982) to issue #120 (May 1983). You took part in panels at VCON 10 in 1982 (PROPAGANDA IN SF, along with Evelyn Beheshti, Steve Wodz and Ed Hutchings, plus THE PUBBUG STRIKES BACK with Robert Runte, Fran Skene and Lari Davidson). Not to mention the earlier SWILLS and a bunch of other fanac. Once a fan, always a fan. "Death will not release you."

But cynicism may... To be honest, I don't know where I fit any more and in writing this issue, ceased to care. When you think of it fandom has been debating who is and who isn't a fan since at least the 1930's, with no resolution in sight...

In issue #15 you devoted a great deal of thought to defining the various types of current fandom, namely 'Traditional', 'Active', 'Digital', and 'Genre consumers.' I don't dispute these labels, they are as convenient and useful as any. But why bother with labels, some may ask? You can't debate what fandom is and was without terms defining this or that approach or purpose within fandom. The trouble is, everyone has to agree on what the various labels mean, and they don't.

Recently traditional fandom has been active on a number of Facebook sights debating the meaning and function of traditional fandom. Labels like 'Fandom,' 'Faandom,' 'Trufen,' etc. are tossed into the fray to no good result because of two problems: 1) there are too damn many terms and when you confront a neofan with one they've never heard of, you have to pause to explain, and 2) explanations vary according to the explainer's individual take on fandom. This tends to create circular arguments based on thorough misunderstanding. No wonder it's hard to attract neofen into the fold. The old pharts give the impression they don't know what they're talking about, or at the very least, have a mindset of a positively Byzantine nature (forever arguing over how many angels can dance on the head of a pin, as it were...) In other words, the baggage of traditional fandom acts as an impediment to recruitment. Sad, but there it is.

I agree. And I choose not to side with Byzantium...

Being as obsessed with promoting fanzine publishing as I am, I've decided to divest myself of as much as the baggage as possible and simplify, simplify, simplify... I intend to stick to the following three terms:

FANDOM: Anybody who likes SF&F stuff.

ZINEDOM: Them as loves the art of publishing SF&F fanzines.

OLD FANDOM: Those who still cherish the lore and practices of early fandom.

Yep, I think that I will play with these from now on as major categories of fandom, with sub-categories within each. With two changes... FANDOM: Anybody who likes SF&F stuff and self-identifies themselves as a fan. GENRE CONSUMER: Anybody who likes SF&F stuff.

Naturally all three terms encompass each other to some degree, but you will note I divorce Zinedom from Old Fandom. This allows me to concentrate on Zinedom as a current, contemporary phenomenon free of historical baggage. I feel this is very necessary if fresh recruits are to be attracted.

I agree absolutely.

Mind you, I will still sprinkle arcane faanish terms throughout my promotional writings in the hope it might spark an interest within readers in past traditions, but when it comes to proselytizing mundanes into zinefen, the above three terms will be the only labels I will use.

Lester Rainfield's two paragraph description of the act of 'Pissing on a Pile of Old Amazings' is quite lyrical and the best part of his article. The rest, admonishing readers to ignore Virtual Reality literature, is wasted on me, since I have no idea what he's talking about. Never assume a reader is *au courant* in

SF lit. I certainly am not. I echo Lloyd Penney's assertion that there is little in modern SF to attract old-time readers like myself who imprinted on SF stressing 'sense of wonder' as opposed to the darker 'sense of impending doom' so prevalent today which, as you point out, merely reflects contemporary knowledge that the future will be worse than current reality, not better.

I still think there are 'sense of wonder' works being done, but they tend to contain some elements of darkness too. I don't know if anyone is still publishing happy-happy, things will only get better and better stories.

On to SWILL #16:

On your editorial re the idiocy of the Conservatives in America, I note their current mantra is "The only way to stop a bad guy with a gun is a good guy with a gun." What they fail to mention is the reverse is equally true, hence the recent spate of cops being killed or wounded while 'attempting' to take out bad guys. The NRA seems to assume criminals are incompetent with guns. Taint necessarily so.

Besides, many bad guys were good guys all along, taking proper training courses, proud members of the NRA, etc., but when they impulsively decide to kill their families or whatever, are magically transferred to the bad guy status without any reference to their former good guy status. Anybody keeping tabs on how many members of the NRA commit criminal actions fatal to their victims? That's one stat I'd love to see.

Furthermore, any society which encourages its members to treat each other as potential enemies rather than fellow citizens is doomed to failure. No wonder they're in decline.

Me, I believe only police, the armed forces, hunters, farmers, and sports target shooters should own guns, with the most powerful being reserved strictly for the first two categories. I firmly believe in the concept of communal citizenship (one for all, all for one) where accepting neighbours as fellow citizens is taken for granted, where criminals are viewed as the exception and not the presumed norm. Rather than blather on and on, I will simply state that I firmly believe our Canadian system is superior to the American system. Period.

We are both in strong agreement on this issue and I also prefer the Canadian Way...

Re: your comments on Taral's comments. The only thing Taral is guilty of is being convinced that he's right. I envy that. I tend to stumble along wondering if I know what the hell is going on. I'm not always convinced that I am right in my views, but tend to be convinced I am usually not entirely wrong. It works for me.

Taral is easily as passionate about zinedom and old fandom as I am, probably more so, but has his own perspective on things (as do I). That said, I thought you defended yourself rather well. In fact, one of the useful aspects of Taral's criticism is that it produced your explanatory outburst wherein you clearly define yourself and your purpose, and that's a good thing. Differences of opinion expressed in endless debate is both a virtue and a curse for Old Fandom, but is very much a cornerstone of same. I wouldn't have it otherwise.

I really don't get old fandom. As I have mentioned in previous SWILLs, it was really before my time when I arrived on the scene in the 1970s. It persisted, fairly strongly, but it was a closed club, no open to new members. I certainly wouldn't define it as the majority group within SF fandom; it hasn't been that for a few decades at least.

SFContario 2012 must have been a real horror show for Lester. There were aspects of the con he actually liked! What a bummer! Sort of spoils the intent of his article. Still, there are the Old Fandom fans to fall back on as a target. That most of them haven't changed in decades is of course correct, but that's a human failing, most adults stop changing once they become adult. It takes much effort to embrace change, it needs to be the hobby of choice, and most people prefer other hobbies. In my case I choose to be a retro fan, a twentieth century kinda guy, and reject modern times as irrelevant to my enjoyment of life. I'm not entirely brain dead though, I remain intrigued with change, but prefer to be an observer rather than a participant. Ghu knows what Lester makes of that, but I is what I is. Anyway, I enjoyed his report.

Lester is Lester, what can I say... Actually, he likes this con and it is the only one he attends regularly – he's been to all three and I've only been to the most recent two. Lester will either give me a LoC to your LoC or use your comments as material in one of his columns.

Re: the Leninski reprint: one slight flaw, 'Dirigible' does not mean 'not rigid'. The one thing that distinguishes a dirigible from other airships (like blimps for instance) is that it possesses a rigid internal framework. However, the basic point that a kilometre long airship travelling at 500 km/hr would tear itself to pieces is quite correct. In fact, the whole review of THE PROBABILITY BROACH is bang on. 'Preaching to the converted' indeed, only nowadays this has been extended to journalism, alas.

Actually, you are both wrong. 'Dirigible' means capable of being steered, controlled, or directed; literally from the Latin it means able to be directed.

Not all Americans are idiots by the way, just the ones who've taken the American concept of individualism to the level of crank extremism. Most of the others are rather decent blokes I believe.

In his LoC Lloyd writes: *"In the long run, you've got to find the fun you want."* Absolutely, when it stops being fun and becomes a burden, it's time to gafiate. It occurs to me that one of the advantages of the increasing diversity of fandom is that there is more to pick and choose from. The multiplicity of choices is not a catastrophe, but a blessing methinks. Certainly an opportunity.

On a personal note, I've grown increasing tired of the ephemeral nature of Facebook communication and debate. Here today, gone in the next few minutes. Not very satisfying. I'm toying with switching to LoC writing instead. I may become a SWILL regular. Call it a New Year's resolution.

Cheers! Graeme

You are more than welcome to become a SWILL regular. Next deadline for your column is June 16th. Neil

Endnote: Nom de Plume

James William Neilson

So, here is where I was supposed to trash the winner of last
year's poll, Ad Astra. This will not happen. Is Ad Astra not
worthy of being trashed? Maybe it is, maybe it isn't. I have
other topics more important to address.

The more observant of our readers will have noticed that nothing
in this issue has been written by Neil Jamieson-Williams, not
even this Endnote. All of the contents of this issue have been
written by the editor and publisher of this zine, except, as
always, the column by Lester Rainsford. There are some of our
readers who believe that Lester is just one of my pseudonyms
which is incorrect (Those who attended SFContario 3 may have
actually met him, in person). Unless an article was a
collaboration between SWILL contributors, the editor and
publisher has always used his real, legal name, until now.

My employer (I endeavour, as per orders by my employer, not to
make my employer public and therefore emphasise my Lecturer
status at McMaster University; most of my teaching load has been
assigned, by my actual employer, to McMaster. I am stating this
as I want to make clear that the policy I am about to discuss is
NOT a McMaster policy.) is not a university and in Ontario, only
university faculty have any academic freedom (okay, since the
most recent government imposed contract, Ontario secondary school
teachers now have limited academic freedom). For the past five
years my employer has prohibited me from making use of my
academic affiliation for any and all forms of publication
(academic, fiction, and non-fiction) or when presenting at
conferences/congresses/conventions/symposia. I have endured this
and found some work-arounds, but for academic, peer-reviewed
publications, they do not work. It did allow me to present at a
handful of conferences, which I did until recently.

What changed? My employer has instituted a new policy regarding their brand and brand protection. Under this policy long term employees (currently not specified but I've been working at this particular institution for over 12 years) and their legal names are considered to be associated brands to the employer and therefore the employer has some control as to how the employee uses that associated brand, in particular, if the employee uses the associated brand in a manner that may negatively impact the employer's brand.

Thus, if any employee (not just faculty) writes, say a letter to the editor that advocates that the Tar Sands should not be further developed, and that letter gets published in a newspaper, using the employee's real, legal name; they are in big trouble. Some of our corporate partners are in the petroleum industry; some of our partners are major donors to the Conservative Party of Canada, etc. This letter to the editor could be perceived as an associated brand harming the major brand. Penalty for violation, immediate termination. In all probability, this policy wouldn't stand up under the collective agreement, or the legal system; however, both of those systems for redress take years.

And so, this zine is now edited and published by James William Neilson. Mr. Neilson also writes textbooks, fiction, and academic works. James William Neilson will be attending SFContario 4 later this year and probably also Ad Astra 2014.

How was my associated brand being detrimental to my employer's brand? The most recent subculture that I had studied were Modern Pagans (previous groups being particle physicists, software developers, open mike musicians, BBS communities) and I am currently researching science fiction fandom and science fiction writers. According to my employer, I "only study freaks and weirdoes" and therefore the subject material of my research and publications are potentially harmful to the employer's brand.

CODA

A list of SWILL volumes:

Original SWILL	issues 1 through 7
SWILL 2011	issues 8 through 12
SWILL 2012	issues 13 through 17
SWILL 2013	issues 18 through 22
SWILL 2014	issues 23 through 26
SWILL 2015	issues 27 through 30
SWILL 2016/2017	issues 31 through 35
SWILL Annuals: Volume 1	issues 36 through 40

Vile Fen Press

a division of Klatha Entertainment an Uldune Media company

www.ingramcontent.com/pod-product-compliance
Lightning Source LLC
Chambersburg PA
CBHW081256040426
42452CB00014B/2518